Educational Philosophy of Mahatma Gandhi and Vinoba Bhave

L.M. BHOLE
Professor of Economics (Retd.)
IIT, Mumbai

SHIPRA

Rs. 995

ISBN: 978-81-7541-880-6

First Published in India in 2017

Educational Philosophy of Mahatma Gandhi and Vinoba Bhave

Published by:

SHIPRA PUBLICATIONS
LG 18-19, Pankaj Central Market,
I.P. Ext., Patparganj, Delhi 110092, India
Ph.: 011- 2223 5152, 2223 6152
Email: info@shiprapublication.com
www.shiprapublication.com

Acknowledgements

Gandhiji once said, 'I have nothing new to tell to the people'. This applies hundred-fold strongly to this book. While Gandhiji's statement expresses pure, simple, genuine humility, the same cannot be claimed in the case of this book. There is little original in this book in respect of position, method, and yet it is being presented before the public because it was felt that it may play a role similar to the role a little squirrel played in the Ramayana. There has also been a motive of "svantah sukhaya". I wanted to study further the Gandhi-Vinoba thought. My wish coincided with the wish of Shri D. Kumarji of Shipra Publications, who suggested that I should write a book on Gandhian philosophy of education. It was a situation of "Yellower than Gold" (*sonyahoon pivale*) or "Sugar in milk" (*Doodhat sakhar*), and I readily accepted his suggestion. I am highly indebted to Shri D. Kumarji, Shipra Publications, for reposing confidence in me, and inducing me to write this book.

While writing this book, I have made a liberal use of writings of Gandhiji and Vinobaji, and also the papers and articles available from the Internet, all of which I could not include in References, because they are too many. There is also a difficulty that quite often the references available through Internet do not give details uniformly and completely. I owe a heavy burden of debt to all those anonymous writers. My debt to the great teachers and authors from India and abroad is obvious and absolute. I am very much thankful to Prof. D. Parthasarathy, Head, Dept. of Humanities and Social Sciences, Indian Institute of Technology, Mumbai for making funds available to me to meet the expenses incurred for preparing the manuscript of the book.

I must thank Mr. Kunju Kunju who sweated to make out my bad handwriting and transform untidily kept notes into, as far as possible, error-free manuscript. I appreciate his help of various kind to me.

L.M. Bhole

Contents

1

Introduction

Education is a double-edged instrument. Good education is the greatest asset. It is a useful resource; it can be instrumental in saving the human civilization which is rushing post-haste towards its own extinction or the bad education, on the other hand, is bound to yield bitter fruits. The world-wide trends in education have been predominantly negative. Two mutually interactive trends have developed, namely, the crisis of survival of whole mankind and the crisis of education. The man has been waylaid by the sparkle, blaze, glint of modern civilization that has robbed mankind of its humanity, humaneness. On the other side, good education could have been the redeeming factor. The good education could have revolutionized itself or it would have halted the decline in civilization. Unfortunately, both these things have not taken place. The end result has been: (a) The crisis of survival of humanity; (b) The crisis of education; (c) The universal, pandemic pathology of developments.

It is not that no efforts have been made at all to improve the state of education in India and abroad. The scientists, social scientists, and others have undertaken efforts to improve the state of education in the world. But these efforts have been about peripherals, superfluous matters, they have involved some reforms but not radical and revolutionary in nature. The significant exception to this has been the thought, philosophy on education of Mahatma Gandhi and Vinoba Bhave. Gandhi-Vinoba's work and experiments on education have been exceptionally fundamental, original, deep, relevant, appropriate, redeeming and revolutionary. However, in India also, the people—citizens, leaders, policy makers, educationists and so on—have not heeded to the wise, potentially effective suggestions. Due to "poverty of ideas", due to "failure of implementation", due to non-acceptance of Gandhi-Vinoba's ideas out of jealousy, pride, hubris, politicization, superiority complex, and vested interests, the educational revolution has remained a non-starter in India also.

It is in this context that the present book seeks to discuss, explain the educational philosophy of Gandhi-Vinoba (G-V). It seeks to be helpful in alleviating the pathological condition of education, and to improve the health of education with the help of philosophy, vision, and mission of G-V. In this book, we wish to study Gandhi-Vinoba's philosophy of education. This is an endeavour to exegesis of educational philosophy of G-V. The book wishes to review, resurrect, apply and implement educational philosophy of G-V. It discusses questions such as the following: What is Nai Talim (NT–New Education) and what has been its progress? What are the major tenets of educational philosophy of Gandhi-Vinoba? What policy suggestions can be given so that appropriate educational system for India can evolve at the earliest? The book also briefly traces the evolution of Indian education system (IES) during the period of Ancient to modern India. It also presents the inadequacies, drawbacks, faults, etc. of present IES. Such discussions are valuable and necessary because the past background helps to understand better the present and future. This also discusses various institutions, super-structural contents and other prerequisites which would define the nature, content, shape of New Education.

Some educationists in the world have pointed out many issues which are demanding solutions urgently. For example, (a) There is an anxiety that the modern education is adrift without rudder, chart or compass, (b) The educational aims are vague and conflicting, and they would not generate strong loyalty, (c) There has been a serious let down in standards of education, (d) The public does not appear to be sure of their deterministic conception of education. Therefore, the objectives of this book, stated in itemized fashion are:

(a) To discuss a very important theme, namely, philosophy of education of the truly great seers and educationists, namely, Mahatma Gandhi and Vinoba Bhave.

(b) To resurrect, revive and spread the interest and commitment of the people in the world in Gandhi-Vinoba's thought.
(c) To discuss the educational side of *Sarvodaya* Revolution.
(d) To document the faults, distortions which have come to afflict the Indian Educational System.
(e) To suggest measures, policies for building a healthy, alternative Educational System for India.
(f) To study, explain, discuss the educational thought of Gandhi-Vinoba and thereby to sustain the emerging interest in education.

Next only to God-realization, the goal of man is to be "anandi", happy, "sukhi". The prayers are for happiness. The blessings are for happiness. We say, "*Sukhi Bhava*".

(1) The Marathi Saint-Poet, Dnaneshwara had the aspiration,

Avaghachi Sansar Sukhacha Kareen
Aanande Bharin Tihi loka

[It means I will make the whole world happy; I will fill all the three *lokas* with pleasure.]

(2) Then there is a *Vedic Shanti* (peace) Mantra:

Sarve bhavantu sukhinah
sarve santu niramayaah
Sarve bhadrani pashyantu
ma kashchid duhkhamaapnuyat.

[It means, let everyone (all) be happy;
Let everyone (all) be healthy
Let everyone (all) see good things,
Let no one be unhappy]

(3) *Brahma Satyam*

Jagat Mithya
Jivanam Satya Shodhnam

[It means, only the Brahma is true or *Satya*, this world is false, life is for realizing *Satya* (Brahma)].

(4) *Asato Ma Sadgamaya*

Tamaso Ma Jyotirgamaya
Mrityormamritam Gamaya

[It means, O'God, lead me from untruth to truth, from darkness to light, and from death to deathlessness.]

(5) *Om Sahna va vatu, sah nau bhunaktan*
Sahaviryam Karvavaha, tejaswinam vadhi tasmsta
Ma vidvisha vahe
Om Shantihi, Shantihi, Shantihi !

[It means, O'God, protect both of us (teacher and pupil). Look after us. Guide us so that we stay together, and perform divine, brilliant, spiritual acts. Bless us so that we do not hate each other.]

(6) To angels the God's throne
To insects, the sensual lust.

(7) Ravindranath Tagore has presented a beautiful poem about the state of mind, i.e., what should be the state of mind that is required. A few lines are given below.

Anter mam vikasit karahe
Nirmal kar ujwal karhe Nirbhay karahe.

One of the sources of Gandhi-Vinoba has been Isavasya Upanishad.

The following shlokas are very useful in understanding G-V philosophy:

(8) *Andham tamha pravishanti Ye Avidyam Upasate*
Tato bhuya evate tamo ya Woo Vidyam rataha

[They who worship *Avidya* (rites) enter into blindering darkness, and they, who are engaged in *Vidya* (meditation) verily fall, as though, into an even greater darkness.]

(9) *Anyadevahur vidyaya anyadahura Vidya*
Iti shushrum dhiranam ye nastad Vichachakashire | |

[One thing, they say, is verily obtained from *Vidya*, another thing they say from *avidya*; thus, we have heard from the wise who explained that to us.]

(10) *Vidhaym cha avidyam cha yastada vedobhayam saha* |
Avidya mritum tirtwa vidya amritam anushnate | |

> [He who knows at the same time both *Vidya* and *Avidya* , overcomes death by *Avidya* and obtains immortality by *Vidya*.]

In the discussion in this book, we would be studying the different definitions of education. We would find that education is defined as *vidya*. It is said that education imparts knowledge. In day-to-day life, the terms *dnan, admyan, vidnan, sadnan, vidya, avidya* are used, and quite often they are used to convey wisdom or some truth. For example:

(1) *Dnanm, paramam dheyam* (knowledge is the supreme goal).
(2) *Vidya vinayen shobhate* (*Vidya* appears beautiful by humility).
(3) *Nahi dnanen sadrusham paritramina vidyate* (there is nothing sacred as dnan).
(4) *Nasti vidya samam chakshu*. (There is no other eye like the *Vidya*.)
(5) *Sa vidya ya vimuktaye* (That which liberates is *vidya*.)
(6) *Dnanam tritiyam manujasya netram* (*dnan* is man's third eye).
(7) *Sarvasya lochanm Shastruyasya nasti antham eva saha* (The one who does not have *dnan* is blind.)

The above-given discussion of *dnan, vidya* should enable us to understand the field of education and education policy-making better. What should be noted is that there are two types of dnan; it has two natures: one, *dnan, satyam*; two, *avidya*.

Thus, education is a valuable, important factor or variable in the life of the individual and in nation-building. However, it remains valuable only if and only when it contributes for the growth, development, and social change of societies, i.e., it helps men to progress towards the destiny of man. If education is harnessed entirely or even primarily to attain only the mundane matters or materialism, it tends to become useless. Education must not be evaluated only on the basis of material advancement. Jobs or employment creation, money-making, affluence cannot be the primary goals of education. In short, education has two aspects, namely, material and spiritual; education sans the latter is incomplete, it is a parody of education. The value of education without spirituality is only zero.

What is the need for education? Best of the education is necessary for the progress of soul. In life (while living, leading life) our various actions (karma) result in some or other *"paap"* or sin. Knowledge, education sharpens our viewpoints, it increases our power of thinking, it teaches us what is right and what is wrong.

Accordingly to the philosopher E. Kant, 'the man can become only through education.'

Victor Hugo has said, 'one who opens the door of the school closes the prison.'

John Dewey, the American sociologist has opined that 'education is not preparation of life, it is life itself'.

Will Durantt, again a philosopher has said that 'education is the transmission of civilization'.

Nunn has defined 'education as a practical philosophy'.

Fichte has said that 'the art of education will never attain complete cleaners in itself without philosophy'. (*Also see* Appendix).

On the basis of the authority of the masters, we can accept that education is a valuable process through which man becomes man. The value of education diminishes the impoverishment of the goals of education occurs. If education is entirely or primarily oriented towards money making, becoming rich or affluent, its value would diminish.

The spirituality must be very much a live concern in education. It can be clearly seen from the above that there is a wide gulf in the views of different educationists. While some are in favour of opening schools, the others would like to close them down.

F.F. Schumacher, an economist, has said human civilizations were built, they flourished for some time, then they decayed, ultimately collapsed and perished, and they then were rebuilt again. In building the civilization anew, the education played an important role. The education is a valuable factor in the process of growth development, social change, etc. Even college and University-going students hate education chores. Therefore, someone may define education as punishment.

The chapter-scheme of the book is as described below:

Chapter One introduces the theme of the book. It refers to the crisis of survival of human civilization, and the crisis of education. Chapter Two describes the personalities of Mahatma Gandhi and

Vinoba Bhave respectively. Chapter Three presents the state of education in India during Vedic, Buddhist, and Muslim periods or eras. Chapter Four discusses the educational conditions, salient features, the inadequacies, faults, drawbacks, shortcomings, and failures of the Indian education in the recent past. Gandhi-Vinoba's general contribution to educational theory, practice, and perspective are discussed in Chapter Five. The New Education or Nai Talim as it has evolved in India, in Chapters six and seven. Educational revolution through Acharyakul, and Gandhi and Vinoba on teachers and students are discussed in Chapter Eight and Nine, respectively. The Appendix at the end of the book contains "Suvarna vichar kana" or "Suvarna vichar bindu" (Golden thoughts) from Gandhiji, Vinobaji, and other scholars. The efforts to gather and compile them were taken because it was felt that researchers, writers, and others would find it useful and convenient to use this source. A systematic study of these "*sutra*-like" "vichar kana" would help to arrive at educational philosophy of Gandhi-Vinoba.

This book is a combined presentation of the educational philosophy of both Mahatma Gandhi and Vinoba Bhave. The complementarity and supplementarity to each other has been of so high a degree that it may be said that there exists a near unity or "*advait*" between them. As a result, there is some advantage in studying, conveying their views, their thought in a combined manner. This thought or rationale induced us to determine the scope of this study to be what it actually is.

The educational philosophy of Mahatma Gandhi and Vinoba Bhave which is the focus of attention in this book is inspired by the scriptural, spiritual wisdom of India which is expressed in innumerable sources, viz. Vedas, Upanishads, Puranas, etc. All of them cannot be reproduced here. What can, however, be done is to refer to a few of them as examples. This is what has been actually done in this book.

2

Life and Work Profile of Mahatma Gandhi and Vinoba Bhave

Gandhiji was born on October 2, 1869, lived a tremendously full, busy, engaged life of service till the Heavens called him back on January 30, 1948. He passed Matriculation in 1887, and left India for England. His full name was Mohandas Karamchand Gandhi, but for crores of people, he was a "Bapu" or the Father of Nation or Rashtrapita. His first name was Mohan which was the name of Lord Shri Krishna who is called Jagadguru or Yogiaancha Yogi or a "Stitpradnya".

Vinoba was born at Gagode, a small village in Konkan, Maharashtra State in India on September 11, 1895. His full name was Vinayak Narhari Bhave. He was variously addressed by different people as Vinaya (particularly by his mother Rukmini), Vinoba, Baba, and Acharya. His mother expired at the young age of 42 years on October 24, 1918. Vinoba's own "Mahanirvan" took place on November 15, 1982.

The seeds of renunciation which we see in Vinoba's life were sown in his childhood. It is amazing that he took the vow of Brahmacharya at the early age of 10 years old. Vinoba passed Matric examination in 1913 after which he never looked back to formal education.

Gandhiji and Vinobaji had a great influence, power over the masses. In their company many people transformed themselves from ordinary being into heroes overnight. They had an uncanny power to coin new words or terms which were replete in meaning and messages, viz., Samyayoga, satyagraha, *sarvodaya*, Gram *Swaraj*. The secret of their power was their faith or belief in Advait philosophy (He all in him and him in all).

Gandhi-Vinoba are the contemporary examples of stitpradnya. They have given many unique gifts to India and other countries. For example, the daily regular prayers at the individual and collective or *samuhic* prayers, they used to advise that social workers and others also must pray daily. The prayers became an essential, integral part of Gandhi-Vinoba's Ashrama, political, social, life. During the last few years of their revolutionary struggle, prayers became legendry in which lakhs of people attended their morning-evening prayer meetings.

In their philosophy, they give a definite emphasis on the observance of 12-13 "*vratas*" for the purification of life. *Vratas* have been talked about earlier also, but not with such imperativeness. In the past, the need for *vratas* was for "Sadhakas" only. Gandhi-Vinoba insisted that the observance of *vratas* is inescapable for everyone, sadhaks and ordinary folks in daily mundane life also. They insisted that spiritual values are necessary and relevant in social service also. The people think that these *vratas* are a bondage which is not true. There are "*Panchyam*", "*Panchniyam*", to which G-V added a few "Yama-Niyamas" and gave them the status of "*vratas*".

Vinoba was a famous philosopher, political thinker and social worker. He was also a great educationist. In the present educational environment his ideas about the work and the role of teacher are very important and relevant. Vinobaji regarded *Bhoodan* and *Gramadana* movements as university.

Vinoba was an Acharya. He was a teacher engaging himself in teaching and learning, advising, conducting experiments in education. He called himself a teacher in his whole life. He was an advocate of "*Sahaj*", "Moolodyoga-backed education". The aim of education is *Mukti*. A few adjectives highlighting the qualities of Vinoba are: Spiritual pragmatist, Saint, Spiritual revolutionary, Samanvayacharya, Drashta, Bhashyakar, Shastri, "Krantdarshi", Sutrakar.

Vinoba can be said to have been a master of vows. At the tender age of 10, he took the vow of "*Brahamacharya*" for life. He possessed extra-ordinary strength to fulfill the vows taken. He believed that the goal of life was "*Satya*", the method of life was self-discipline, and the life-work was service. Renunciation, sacrifice, service, self-control were important values according to Vinoba.

Sane Guruji, Gandhiji, Vinoba are only a few examples of how mothers make spiritual giants. It is through his mother that Vinoba learnt the following gems of thought:

(i) The one who gives is *Deo* 'God', and the one who withholds is a demon.
(ii) The Sweetness is in having a little.
(iii) There is a cheating in having more.
(iv) We should get enough food and clothes, more than that is not needed.

Vinoba used to say that he was his mother's son. Nobody else has influenced his life as his mother has. No one else had a power over him as his mother had. Vinoba was a voracious reader. He has said that literally he had read thousands of books in various languages. Vinoba has given a few interesting facts about his attire or clothes in the early phase of his life. He and his friends used to wear only a "*laṅgoti*" till they were 9-years old. Vinoba joined Sabarmati Ashrama in 1916. Gandhi had a great faith in Vinoba's Spiritual knowledge and wisdom. Vinoba received unstinted praise from Gandhi who used to consult him whenever he was in doubt about his understanding of any part of scriptures. According to Gandhi, Vinoba was a great asset to the Ashrama; he gave much to the Ashrama, but took little from it. Those who knew Vinoba well did think that he was one of the greatest persons in the world in the present age. He was like a "*Vedic Rishi*". Vinoba is said to have been a "Vichar Purush" (man devoted to thought). He had a limitless "Shabda-Shakti", the word-power or words-strength.

Gandhi told the people of India about Vinoba the following: "He (Vinoba) is a Sanskrit Pundit. He revolutionized spinning by using "*takli*". There is absolutely no trace of untouchability in his heart. He believes in communal harmony or communal unity. He had studied holy Koran in original in order to understand the subtleties of Islam."

All languages, cultures, traditions have sung very high praises in favour of their mothers. The mother's love, service, etc. have been eulogized and acknowledged by all. A dry person (only apparently dry) like Vinoba also became quite sentimental, emotional while talking about his mother. There is a saying in Marathi which says, "Jichya hati Palanyach dori ti jagate uddhari" which broadly means that the one who has the rope of cradle in her hands uplifts the world.

Vinoba was Gandhi's closest, reliable, scholarly disciple and colleague at the Ashrama. But because of his shy nature, he avoided coming into limelight, and remained relatively in more or less oblivion. Therefore, when Gandhi announced to the Nation that in the individual Satyagrah which he had decided to launch against the British, Vinoba would be the first individual Satyagrahi.

Vinoba has said that "I am a *fakir,* I do not value money much, nor do I value institutions. I value thoughts. The compassion in me is not for individuals, it is for society (samaj). I always live in the atmosphere of God, continuously converse with God internally. God has given me far more than what I deserve. I am, therefore, immensely grateful to Him". About himself, he further said:

My life has been contemplative. The aim of that contemplation was to discover the roots of social transformation. On one side Gramadan, on the other side, Universal kingdom (Vishwarajya).

> Jai Jagat is our Mantra
> Gramadan is our method
> World peace is our aim.

Gandhi-Vinoba have expressed their vision, mission, paradigm, model of social reconstruction in completely new terms, new ideas, concepts, and philosophy. They replaced the conventional terms such as democracy (*Lokshahi*), Socialism (*Samajvad*), Communism (*Samyavad*), democratic socialism (*Lokshahi samajvad*) by *Swaraj, Hind Swaraj, Gram Swaraj, Gramavad, Antyodaya, Sarvodaya, Samyayoga,* and Decentralization are the terms coined by them.

Gandhi-Vinoba regarded "Brahmacharya" as the important *vrata*. It means continence a life-style which helps the individual to attain "Brahma".

The Coming Age is mine, not of political leaders. The big leaders of big parties will fall and like leaves, as it happens in the season of falling leaves. They do not realise this truth because they are in growing mood. They have Government authority, power is in their hands. They are using that power. They are riding a horse, but the tether is not in their hands.—Vinoba

In Vinoba's views, Gandhi was a great man of exceptionally high level; he was social scientist on par with writers of Smritis. The doubts have been raised as to whether Gandhi was a spiritual being or a political activist. The politics was a facade, playground, turf for his experiments in Truth or God or "Brahmadnyan" or "Aatmadnyan" or "*Aatma sakshatkar*" or "*Moksha*". And all this applies quite well to Vinoba also. Both were endowed with extremely sharp intellect. An honest study of both of them compels one to admit that we had here two persons in the same Age who can be described as revolutionaries, "drashtas", Krantadarshi. If the people had shown sagacity, humility, wisdom, and if they had really walked on the path shown by them, the human kind would have been living on heavenly planet. The proud man has, instead, brought the mother earth to the brink of disaster.

The seeds of fierce renunciation which we see in Vinoba's mature life were sown in the childhood itself.

About himself, Gandhi has said, 'I admit my limitations. I have no university education worth the name. My high-school career was never above the average. I was thankful if I could pass my examinations. During the days of my education, I had read particularly nothing outside text books. I cannot therefore claim much book knowledge. However, I believe I have not lost much due to the enforced restraint. On the contrary, the limited reading may be said to have enabled me to digest thoroughly what I did read.'

'Life is but an endless series of experiments. If my any action claimed to be spiritual, proved to be unpractical, it must be pronounced to be a failure. I do believe that the most spiritual act is the most practical in the true sense of that term.'

Gandhi loved his country, people, and culture, took pride in them. He was a nationalist bounded by universalism; but if choice has to be made between India and Truth, he said, he would be for Truth. He taught us national self-respect and freed us from the intellectual bondage of the West. He inspired us with his new dreams visions, and revolutionized our ways of living and thinking. The love and service of his people was his Dharma.

Gandhi had many friends from abroad. One of them was Romain Rolland. Rolland and Gandhi had a very delightful, and non-conventional relationship. Romain Rolland (RR) was older by four years than Gandhi, and yet he put Gandhi at father's level. RR put himself in position as a son and a disciple. He used to refer to Gandhi as "our master", "the holiness of the master", and the "Guru". RR used to say that Gandhi was better than himself, that he was normally inferior to Gandhi. He had a very fascinating and complex relationship with the masses who venerated and worshipped him as a God. This was so not because of any promises or any demagogic tricks or misleading "oratory". The relationship between Gandhi and intellectuals was, however not always pleasant.

Faced with civilizational crisis, a search for Alternative World Order is going on in all countries. Many thinkers and civilizational guides have come to the conclusion that Gandhi-Vinoba—Alternative is the only alternative today which can help to avert the said survival crisis. Let us see what Martin Luther King, Jr. has said on this point.

He lived as per his philosophy of "Minimization of wants". We are told that in ancient India, Rishis, Yogis, Sanyasins went on reducing their wants progressively till they decided to use no more than a cup of two hands for drinking water. Gandhiji is one of the most important exponents of this virtue. His discarding of clothes till only the lion-cloth remained, the episodes in his life regarding the use of a small branch of Neem tree for cleaning of his teeth and mouth; his experiment to reduce the water needed for cleaning oneself after going to toilet show that his simplicity was not for creating dramatic approach. His experiments in life, his experiments in truth were accompanied by experiments in Arts. He was the least dramatic of individuals. With his lion-cloth, steel-rimmed glasses, rough and hard sandals, long stiff, toothless winning smile and laughter, and voice hardly above whisper, he laughingly wore the epithets such as mad man, faddist, naked fakir hurled by the ignorant.

He used stone instead of soap for his bath, he wrote his letters on little bits of pieces of paper, he wrote with little stumps of pencil which he could hardly hold with his fingers, he shaved with a crude country razor, and ate with a wooden spoon from a prison's bowl.

Gandhi's deepest strivings were spiritual. He said he did not know any religion other than the religion of activity and more activity. Although the whole world addresses him as "Bapu" and "Father of Nation", it is to be remembered that he possessed capacity to shower maternal love, and he had passion for nursing the sick. He was called by some persons as "Bapu my mother".

Gandhiji had a knack of achieving results of Himalayan proportions from apparently small things. He was the earliest visionary of "Small is beautiful". It is recognized, accepted that he was one of the first leaders who raised the alarm about environmental destruction and ecological decay. Let us note three episodes in his life which prove this point.

First, to begin with, he did not mind accepting flowers whenever they were given to him as a mark of welcome. Soon he realized that by accepting flowers at meetings (which were many) he was contributing to environmental destruction. Therefore, at some stage he stopped accepting flowers, and asked people to welcome him by giving yarn spinned by the hosts.

Second instance occurred in his Ashram. A tender branch or twig of a Neem tree or Babul tree was his tooth brush obtained fresh every day from the surroundings. One day, an Ashramite was asked by Gandhiji to get him the tooth brush he needed. After a while, that person presented himself before Gandhiji with a fairly big branch of Neem tree. Gandhiji was surprised and irritated by this, and asked the said person why he brought such a big branch when only a tiny one was needed. The person said that there are so many Neem trees in the Ashram premises, and why one should object if somewhat big branch was cut for Bapu's needs. Gandhiji made him understand that only one Gandhi is not the user of Neem branches, there are many such users. If we cut such big branches for everyone, soon we would make this earth treeless which is a great threat to the survival of our planet.

The third episode is so awesome, and it makes one feel that Gandhiji would always remain an enigma to us. Gandhiji had spent some time experimenting to find out what is the optimum quantity of water an average person would require to be cleaned after going to toilet. It would be instructive to search for result he had got from archives.

Through his various experiments, his capacity to love expanded, and by the end of his life he was aflame with love. He had insatiable love for mankind. Wonder struck with the heights of his achievements, the people would ask him the secret of his success, the secret of his life. He would tell them in the simplest of words the profoundest truths. Asked for a message, he replied, 'my life is my message.' Asked for his secret of life, he replied, '*Renounce and enjoy*.'

The speech he gave before the House of Commons when he went to England to participate in Round Table Conference, was so compelling and impressive that a few members of audience asked Mahadev Desai, Gandhi's Secretary, as to how Gandhi is able to speak so well for such a long time without any preparation, without any promptings, without any notes? Mahadev Desai has said, Gandhi is an effective speaker because what he thinks, what he feels, what he says, and what he does are all one.

It has been said that Gandhi's personality was full of grandeur or magnificence. He was a great apostle of non-violence and revolution, he was a revolutionary par excellence. He advocated decentralization, small is beautiful, arcadian civilization, *sarvodaya*, samuhik inspiration. The story of life of Gandhiji was heroic, there was a genuine, real, honest transformation from Mohan to Mahatma. But Mahatma shared the destiny of Maharshi Vyas towards the end of his life. The pathos of this disillusionment has been lost on people.

Gandhi-Vinoba called themselves as "Sanatani Hindu", because they believed in Vedas, Upanishads, Puranas, etc. They respected each other for their understanding of scriptures and other literature and interpretation of the "Word". Vinoba has paid a high tribute to Gandhi that if he had not received Gandhi's company, he would not have understood the meaning of *Bhagavad Gita* as he has understood it now. The company, the proximity of Gandhi enabled Vinoba to get a key to opening the store-house of spiritual wisdom, knowledge, *vidya*. He saw the actual practice of philosophy in a better way.

Vinoba had told colleagues in the Ashram that there was a wonderful, striking, awe-inspiring synthesis of revolution and peace in Gandhi's personality, as an apostle of peace.

Gandhi had "Sakshatkar" of Gita's "Karmayoga", and there was unity in internal and external of his beings. Gita's "stitpradnya" is personified in Gandhi and Vinoba. Gandhi—the "stitpradnya", compassionate, affectionate great man (*Mahapurush*)—Satpurush, Social scientist of the order of writers of Smritis, exceptionally great man (*nirala Mahapurush*), in lighter vein, one may say that English dictionary would be inadequate to describe Gandhi-Vinoba. We, however, may choose a thousand names and make "Gandhi Sahastranam" as a substitute.

Gandhi-Vinoba's educational thought and Ashram-thought are unique gifts to the world from India. They developed the ideas, concepts, institutions of Ashramas along with fighting for social and political revolution. In other words, Gandhi developed and run Ashramas. One of their tasks was to analyse the mind to develop it so that there is a psychological help to the socio-political economic revolution in the country.

Gandhi gave to his family the nature of Ashramas. Further, his ideas targeted to make *Grihastashram* into *Sanyasashram* without requiring him or without adopting the attire of the Sanyasin. Both Gandhi-Vinoba had a phenomenal energy which they utilized for working on diverse activities. Their humility, fearlessness, sense of humour, faith in prayer were of high order. Both were the seekers, experimenters in Truth and Ahimsa. Their most important experiments were not in mundane matters; they were in the art of living, how to live meaningfully in the world that is full of violence, conflicts, incessant change. G-V thoughts were not about what need to do, or what they ought to have, they were more about what to be.

It is necessary to always remember that Gandhi-Vinoba contribution to spreading the message of love, truth, compassion, etc. had great originality; unlike in the past, they wanted these values to be practised by the families, groups, tribes, communities, societies, nations, and the world, apart from the individuals.

One aspect of the portrait or profile which cannot be left without a comment is the support, the following which Gandhi received in his struggle for "Swaraj". So, it is nothing less than a miracle that Gandhi achieved what he achieved in spite of covert and overt criticism he had to endure with. Because of internal squabbles, diverse motives, conflicts of interests, he did not have full unstinted support from the Congress party. As far as the rightist and leftist parties are concerned, they made his task more and more difficult. There was communal protest against his philosophy, programmes, policies. The scientists, technologists, and other professionals were not with him. But the masses were with him. It is the support of masses with which he could partly neutralize the opposition.

Both Gandhi and Vinoba lived long life. As they reached advance age, they did not feel that they were getting old, they never felt the burden of advanced age. They felt like being young. They felt energetic. Medical examination had revealed that the power of their respective organs, limbs was stable if not increasing. Gandhi wanted to live for 120 years or so.

As a part of a search for commonalities between Gandhi and Vinoba, we should mention two-three points. Both of them believed that the goal of life is discovering the truth or "Atmasakshatkar". Unlike Adi Shankaracharya, both of them believed that this world is not "maya"; it is a place for "purushartha", the place for "Karmayoga". According to them, the goal was to have "Brahmadnyan", the method of life is self-discipline, and the work of life was service. They had achieved unity—both internal and external.

In keeping with their philosophy of minimization of wants, they always lived frugally. In UK, in order to save bus fare, Gandhi used to walk about 10 miles daily. His expenditure in UK was £2 per month. He started writing when he was in England i.e. when he was 18-19 years old. His pieces of writing were on vegetarianism in earlier years.

About his reading and influence on him, there has been a kind of omission; while the influence of Ruskin, Tolstoy, Thoreau is widely mentioned and acknowledged, the significant fact that it is during his stay in England that he read *Bhagavad Gita*, Edwin Arnold's *Light of Asia*, and *Song Celestial*. It is interesting to note that Gandhi was introduced to religious literature via England and English language.

There is another omission about his life, which is about his law practice. The general information is that he was a failure as a lawyer. In reality, he had failed in practising law when he was a novice. But later on in South Africa, he was a sought after, popular, busy lawyer; he had built a practice of £5000 a year, which was a lot of money in those days. He had also built a big house (villa) for his family.

In Gandhi-Vinoba, the world has witnessed a rare, unique relationship which was affectionate, loving, mutual respect, deep warmth, frank and transparency. There was a spiritual relationship. It would not be wrong to say that it was a divine advaitik relationship in which there were two bodies but one soul. Vinoba has said that it was possible to get both *shanti* (peace) and *kranti* (revolution) at the feet of Gandhiji.

In 1924, Vinoba had devoted some time for studying Economics. In those days, the daily minimum per capita income was two annas. In such conditions, Vinoba had experimented to live daily on the income of 13 paise.

Gandhi-Vinoba's approach to work was one of complete non-attachment. In their words whatever work God wants to take from them, He will take. They did not make any plans. Their whole desire was to become a tool in His hands. Beyond this they did not have any independent desire.

One aspect of their life which cannot be left unmentioned is their walking throughout India. Vinoba, like Gandhiji, kept up the Indian tradition of "charaivati", "charaivati", very much alive. It is well-known that in India in all ages, the great masters, teachers had walked to achieve their goals. The prominent examples are: Buddha, Mahavir, Vivekananda, Shankaracharya, Gandhiji and Vinoba. On an average, Vinoba walked 15 miles or 22 km per day. He walked about 70,000 km in about 10 years apparently for Bhoodan and Gramadana, but the real ultimate purpose was to spread the message of love, satya, compassion, ahimsa, equality, etc.

Gandhiji and Vinoba came to this earth primarily to alleviate, reduce, and eliminate sorrow of the people. In Mahabharata, in her meeting with Lord Krishna, Kunti asked for a boon that she should always experience sorrow, suffering, pain or "dukkha". How does one square us this difference between Kunti on the one hand, and Gandhi-Vinoba on the other? First, there exists the difference of Yuga? Kunti belonged to the "Dwapar Yuga"; while Gandhi-Vinoba belonged to Kaliyuga. Second, Kunti was, perhaps, asking for suffering for herself and not for others. In any case, now our goal cannot be different from the goal of eliminating sorrow. The life of mankind has been full of suffering, sorrow, pain. It was Gandhi-Vinoba who had aspired to make human kind peaceful, happy, and stable. They were working for taking mankind from Kaliyuga to Satyauga. In short, their civilizational goal has been to create a culture of peace and happiness in "Satyauga" (*Satyayuga ki wapacy*).

Gandhiji was called *Nanga Fakir* (naked saint) by Winston Churchill. He was ignorant about the rich traditions in India. Otherwise, he would not have used such words. Gandhi-Vinoba were the perfect examples of "Fakiri". About self, Vinoba has said that he was a fakir, he did not give any value to money and to the formal organization. He valued thoughts. The compassion in him was for the society. Vinoba is widely read by the public, and his books have been widely circulated in the world. *Gita-pravachanam,* one of his books has gone in 100 reprints, it has reached 25 lakh people.

The life-time work of both Gandhiji and Vinoba was to discover the laws of ahimsa. Vinoba has touchingly said, '...by nature he (Vinoba) was a wild animal, but Bapu had made him a domesticated animal. Sitting at his feet, uncivilized person like me has become a servant (*sevak*). I am a very hard-hearted man; someone's death does not affect me, nor does somebody's birth make me happy. If my brother becomes sick, I do not worry over it. But the experiences I gained during Bhoodan/Gramadan padyatra have made me what I am now; they have made me humble'. Vinoba continued, while working in Ashram or out of Ashram, the paramount thought in my mind has been how to solve our social or individual problems through non-violence or Ahimsa?' In his Padyatra for Bhoodan and Gramdan, Vinoba performed great task of education of the people (*Lok Shikshan*). To ask for donation of land or village is not to beg for alms, it is giving "Diksha" to the donor.

Vinoba had further said about himself that '... is something of a mystic in me. As a result, I roam on the earth, but my mind or my brain is at another level. The response of people to my work often made me emotional, the tears come in my eyes when I see people's love for me. The love I got from humans and animals is undescribable, we received far more "daan" (donation) from people, we got more than required, more than necessary. We in all humility, with devotion, salute the people. The physical labour is essential for spiritual progress as much as for healthy body. Let us take a vow that we will take the spade, broom, and other divine, sacred, celestial instruments, and use them as decorative'.

One important point which Vinoba has made at many places, and which we can neglect at our own risk is the primary importance of agriculture. He has argued that land is not only a means to produce more. It is an instrument for worshiping Gods. While cultivating land, one gets an internal joy which we cannot get in any other actions. Continuing on this theme, Vinoba has said that we are not proud of any one particular religion. We are not bound by anyone particular caste or community. To roam freely in the garden of good thoughts is our self-study (*svadhyay*). To digest the good thoughts is our "dharma". To establish harmony among various particularities or to develop *Jai Jagat* (universalism) is our sadhana at the thought level.

He has further said, 'I have been a student in the whole of my life, I have been continuously learning and teaching. I have done many things, but the work of learning and teaching has never been forsaken or discontinued. As far as it is possible, I have tried to work keeping away the body, institutions, and money. I am trying to find out, discover as to how Ahimsa should enter and get acceptance in social life. I am a person who belongs to the other world, my world is different. It is my claim that I have love with me; I do not have "mat" (view) with me. I have thought with me. I am not a contestant for anything. Love and thought have a great strength. The strength lies in love and thought. Do not expect from me the inflexible view-points; I am changing every moment. I am only an individual. There is no label on my forehead. I am not a member of any institution. There is no political party which has touched me. I have relationship of love with the institutions which are a part of constructive works programme. All are mine, and I am of all. I cannot make differentiation in love. I do not want to adopt somebody else's religion, somebody else's thought or views. I want to reduce the sorrow of someone or other. I want to work for establishing peaceful revolution. I have spent (used) many years of my life, my solitude, for contemplation or thinking. My life has been spent in contemplation more than service. No difficulty or problem scares me now. The problem may be big but in my hands, it becomes small. I have been trying to find out how to solve social and individual problems by non-violent means. My inclination is towards the methods of Mahavir. But my work actually is being done as per Buddha's ways. I have received the maximum help from Shankar, Dnandev, and Gandhi. Basically I am like a road that is extremely rough or uneven with stones.' A physically frail but indomitable in spirit, Vinoba walked in all seasons without any stop challenging the weather God to obstruct his yajna. He was rightly called "Samanvayacharya" because he spent his whole life in integrating, in uniting the diversity in any field, explaining the Advait to the masses. His message was that of search for Ahimsa, joining the hearts of people, to love was his "Dharma". *Satya, prem, karuna* sum up his philosophy. As he has said, 'All my work, my whole life has been inspired by the goal, the only goal of uniting, joining the peoples' hearts.'

Like Gandhiji, Vinoba's Sahitya is oceanic, it may be possible to cross the "Bhava sagar" but not the oceanic literature of Gandhi-Vinoba. Vinoba's many books, his thousands of sermons (*pravachanas*) and thousands of papers constituted an ever-flowing Speech-Ganga (Vak-Ganga) and Speech-Yadnya (Vak-Yadnya) which may be compared only with the "Vak-Yadnya" about 700-800 years back by Santa Dnyaneshwar. Vinoba's all walking, talking, wandering, speaking were for establishing peace through revolution, or peaceful revolution, Ahimsak Revolution.

In both scared childhood and courageous mass leadership, it

is Ramanama he used as a weapon of last resort. In later life, he walked with Kings but did not lose the common touch.

Gandhiji's school career was a failure. He wanted to be a doctor but could not become one because of failure. Gandhi became a strong votary or advocate of simplicity of life and minimization of wants, the importance, the value, the necessity of which he was, in a way, forced to learn when he was in England as a student and was enamoured by gentlemanly life style for a while. The period proved to be highly formative because he instilled in himself the values of self-reliance, frugality, physical endurance. One of the great points of Gandhi's strength was his being impervious to ridicule, scorn, etc.

It has been said that service and suffering wanted to take a human form and Gandhi was born. *Bhagavad Gita* was the "Spiritual Reference book" for both Gandhi and Vinoba.

About his own non-violence, Gandhiji has made a very strong claim that he has become incapable of hating any being on our planet. He has said, 'by a long course of prayerful discipline, I have ceased for over 40 years to hate anybody. I make this point in all humility. My non-cooperation has its root in love and not in hatred'.

Gandhiji explains further the nature of Non-violence by saying that Satyagraha is gentle; it must not be the result of anger or malice. It is never impatient, vociferous, and it was conceived as a complete substitute for violence.

Gandhiji used to say, 'we must hate the sin, the evil, not the sinner, evil-doer.' Non-violence is an extremely active force. It has no room for cowardice or even weaknesses. The strength does not come from physical capacity. It comes from an indomitable will. Both Gandhi and Vinoba can be given as the best examples of this formulation.

Vinoba has made a revolutionary change in the meaning of and scope of "daan". He supported the idea of *daan* by invoking Shankaracharya who has said, "danam sanvibhagaha" (equitable distribution) is said to be danam. By conceiving the ideas and methods and programmes known as Bhoodan and Gramadan, he has suggested the non-violent method of eliminating exploitation, creating social order that is equitable and just. After having succeeded in respect of Bhoodan and Gramadan, he taught to apply the ideal of "danam" to wealth (*Sampatti Danam*) "sammati danam", etc.

Gandhiji used to say "my life is an indivisible whole, and all of my activities run into one another, and their origin is in insatiable love for mankind".

The eternal Christ-like humility made Gandhi to make profound statements such as the follows:

'I have nothing new to teach the world. Truth and non-violence are as old as the hills. ... my philosophy, if it may be called by that pretentions name, is contained in what I have said. But you will not call it "Gandhism". I have held faster than ever to the position that Truth may not be sacrificed for anything whatsoever. Those who believe in the simple truth I have laid down can propagate them only by living them.'

It is but natural that Gandhi should have been influenced by many persons, and Gandhi has acknowledged this influence. It is remarkable that he has frankly and lovingly and honestly acknowledged the influence Kasturba, his wife, has exerted on him. He has said that he learnt the theory and method of Satyagraha from her. He has said that he learnt the lesson of non-violence from his wife. "When I tried to bend her to my will, because of her determination to resist, and to be ready for suffering, ultimately made me ashamed of myself.'

Gandhi has been persistently criticized by many that his ideas, methods, programmes were impracticable or utopian, unrealistic. He used to reject this charge saying that he had not the shadow of doubt that any man can achieve what he had achieved if he works and makes the same effort and cultivate the same hope and faith. We can liken this assurance to the assurance given by Krishna in Gita. To recall, Krishna had promised the following:

> *Yada yada hi dharmasya glanirbhavati Bharat*
> *Abhyuthanamdharmasya tadatmanam srujamyaham.*

As stated earlier, Mohan was the name of Krishna as well as Gandhi. It can be said that there was a similarity in the work also of these two Mohans. Both can be said to have been the votaries, advocates of the agrarian civilization. The love for cow was another common point between them. Both had to fight super powers to gain Swaraj. Both were the advocates of Ahimsa. It was the philosophy of both that it is only after all the negotiations have completely failed that war should be used for settling the disputes. No one else has done so much work for the liberation of women as two Mohans. Both of them advocated self-reliance. Thus, if one studies honestly the Life and Work of Gandhi and Krishna, one would find many such common features of character and personality of Krishna and Gandhi.

Who was Gandhi? What was Gandhi? There is no other better way to understand Gandhi than to see him through the discerning eyes of Vinoba.

Gandhi has revived the typical Indian tradition of establishing "Ashramas", but while doing so he transformed the tradition by giving it new meaning, new scope. *Family became an Ashram and Ashram became a family under his leadership.* Without wearing the attire of "Sanyasi" (monk, who has embraced the life of complete renunciation), he transformed "Grihastashram" into "Sanyasashram". It was his aim, his plan that every village should have an "Ashrama". Gandhi has been both revered, worshipped, and reviled. The range of epithets showered on him has been mind-bogglingly wide indeed—sage, saint, prophet, genius, crank, faddist and so on. He was called Christ, Mohamad, Buddha, Mahavir, Nanak and so on. There has not been any great man whose name has not been given to him.

Although, much less known, Vinoba also has elevated himself to the highest pinnacle of character, social service, and "Aatma sakshatkar". He has been called a Sant (saint), Rishi, Acharya, revolutionary, and so forth.

Both Gandhi and Vinoba used to emphasize the importance, value of friendliness (*maitry*). They taught the people that they should not depend on leaders, they should become independent and take decisions on their own (this is known as *netrutva nirsan*, and "Gansevaktvam"). They also taught people to become free from most of the institutions (Sanghatan Mukti). Both had excelled in Karmayoga, Bhaktiyoga, Dnanyoga, and Rajyoga. In death, however, they differed beyond imagination while Gandhi was crucified, Vinoba died by his own will (*Swecheha maranam*).

The rapport between the people/masses and G-V was very good indeed. While Gandhi was called Bapu, Vinoba was called Baba by the people. Many leaders drew inspiration from them. The present century should be called "the age of Gandhi-Vinoba" rather than the age of the atom.

Both Gandhi and Vinoba were the great walkers. Like the Buddha, Mahavir, Sankaracharya, Vivekananda, etc. they achieved unprecedented greatness in life by living life. The ideas of both of them were dubbed as utopian by the worldly wise. Gandhi has returned this charge by saying that he was an average person and as an average person what he could achieve, anybody else also could do it.

Both Gandhi and Vinoba were great poets (kavis) in a larger sense of that word. They were "Kavis, manishi" Krant darshi. All-religions prayer (*Sarva Dharma prarthana*), the shloka comprising all *vratas*, and Gitai are the examples in this context.

One facet Gandhi-Vinoba's life that has not been sufficiently, widely known is the ability of G-V to make great speeches. They have made innumerable speeches. We refer to three of Gandhi's speeches here.

(i) The first speech was made by Gandhiji in South Africa on September 11, 1906 at Empire Theatre in Johannesburg against the Law for Registration of Africans.
(ii) The second speech was given in Varanasi in 1916 on the occasion of inauguration of BHU.
(iii) The third speech was made on August 9, 1942, at Bombay (now Mumbai). It is now known as "Quit India" speech. Apart from these speeches, as said above, he spoke to a large number of the students, teachers, academics, political events, and political agitations. For example, his speeches (a) in House of Commons in England, (b) in Wardha at Nai Talim Conference in 1937 were epoch-making. He was an effective speaker but not like Hitler.

The war speeches of Churchill are also quite famous. But while the ultimate aim of Churchill's speeches was to save colonialism and Western modern civilization, Gandhi's speeches were for liquidating colonialism and Modern Western civilization. While Churchill's speeches were emotionally charged and they fomented war psychosis, Gandhi's speeches were educative, urging everyone to end war and return to peace.

Towards creating such a new civilization, their intellect, mind, and intuition gave to the world highly original ideas, philosophy, programmes. For example, Gramaswaraj, Samya Yoga, Gramadan, *Sarvodaya*. Both of them rejected the current concept of freedom, in its place, they gave the ideal of Swaraj which is a very comprehensive idea. Through books such as *Hind Swaraj*, and *Swaraj Shastra*, they tried to explain the full meaning of Swaraj.

Gandhi-Vinoba were both saints and prophets. Both were outstanding personalities. They were called to be revolutionary saints, and spiritual pragmatists.

Gandhi-Vinoba were called 'Father of Nation', 'Father of Non-Violence' and 'Father of Nai Talim'.

Both Gandhi and Vinoba were not individuals, they were thoughts. Both of them were spiritual men. Both of them have produced very vast literature. Both of them took great pride in and loved Indian culture and people. They exerted so that she does not join western or modern civilization. They were there to liquidate the Modern civilization. Both of them were the advocates of rural arcadian civilization; they were "Gramvadi" and not "Samajvadi".

It was Gandhi's originality and intuition that he added completely new things to "Ashram System". He made it flexible. He emphasized greatly the importance of and need for "Brahmcharya". He put forth the idea (and practised it) that "Brahmcharya" can be and should be practised in "Grihastashram" also. Gandhi's high discernment is reflected in his view that what is applicable, what is relevant to the individual is true for the society, collectivity also.

It is known to many that one of Gandhi's traits was to immediately put into practice what one comes to believe in. Gandhi was not any one individual, he had become the pulse, feeling of the entire nation.

The true understanding of Gandhi and Vinoba can be obtained by knowing "the self on self", Gandhi on Gandhi. Both of them have given self-assessment which is most frank, honest, balanced. They have mentioned their demerits (*avagunas*) and merits (*Gunas*). We end these profiles or portraits of G-V with what Gandhiji has said about himself as an example. He had said, 'Just as my success and my "pratibha" (intelligence, splendor of knowledge, intuition) are the gifts of God, my short-coming and failures are also gifts from God. I offer both of them at the feet of God. Why did He choose an imperfect man like me for such a great experiment? I think he must have done so deliberately. I think He wanted to serve crores of dumb poor, and ignorant people. The people perhaps would have been disappointed if they had seen a perfect, poorna being. Therefore, a weak and imperfect person like them who is progressing in the direction of Ahimsa (has been chosen by Him). It is possible that the person who comes after me would be stronger and perfect than me. And you will be capable of accepting his message. For the present, "my life is my message".'

Another best gift India has offered to the world is Ashrama. While working for social, political, spiritual revolution, G-V revived the concept, institution, and organization of Ashrama. Both of them resurrected in the entity of Ashram and used it for laboratory like experimentation in various matters. Another gift which should be mentioned is the concept of "Kshetra Sanyas". In the midst of very active life for Bhoodan and Gramadana, Vinoba lived in one place for 30 years experimenting for "Samya Yoga" through "abhidhyan" or "Abhidhayam" param samyam.

Vinoba was a "spiritual heir" of Bapu. He had a burning fire or burning fervour of revolution in him. But from outside, there was peace, Himalayan peace. Gandhiji has said that Vinoba was one of the few pearls in the Ashram whom he had come to bless, and not to get blessed him by others. Gandhi and Vinoba have been called practical idealist, spiritual pragmatist, revolutionary Saint, Samanvayacharya, and the Greater Walker. According to Vinobaji the aim of education is to realise the spiritual basis of the human endeavours. He laid a great stress on the spiritual and moral foundations of Education. It is about acquiring and distributing knowledge. In India, education has played a very important role in the development of Indian Freedom Struggle. It was through education that India became aware of the knowledge of the West. India has cherished the world of education through many wise people whose basic thought, philosophies enriched the literature on education. Vinoba Bhave has been one of the stars in this galaxy of the wise. Gandhi's intuition enabled him to add completely new things to the Ashram system. He made it flexible, stressed the vrat of Brahmacharya more, held that Brahmacharya should be practised by both individual and "society".

3

Educational System in India during Vedic, Buddhist, and Islamic Periods

Ancient philosophy of education was not in conflict with the philosophy of life. There was no reason for a quarrel between these philosophies. They were complementary to each other and they exerted influence on each other. The ancient life and education in India were "Dharmamaya"—full of Dharma. All the activities in life were replete with Dharma; they were controlled by Dharma.

The objective of this chapter is to provide a bird's eye-view of the nature, scope, the extent of development, socialization of the Indian Educational System (IES) during different periods of time stretching from ancient to the modern. This chapter is meant to provide the background for the discussion of the philosophy of education by Mahatma Gandhi and Vinoba Bhave—the greatest educationists in the world.

Vedic Period

The education in ancient India was an integral part of the Aryan religion. The oldest text-book of religion is Rigveda. The Vedic period includes the periods of Upanishad, Brahmenic, Aranyakist, and Sutra periods. The oldest religious scripture (Rigveda) has given the oldest system of education to the human kind. Rigveda and Yogasutra can be said to be the two earliest text-books on education not only for India but also the whole world. The Rigveda was "seen" and composed by six Rishis namely, Grudsamad, Vishwamitra, Atri, Vashista, Vamadeva and Bhardwaj. The author of Yogasutra was Patanjali. Every Rishi was a teacher. The Rigvedic hymns were (used to be) the first course of study for the student.

Shankaracharya has said,

- *Matru pitru sahasrabhyo Hiteshi vedaha.*
  (It means that vedas are thousand times more beneficial than father and mother)
- Dnaneshwar (a Saint from Maharashtra) has said,
  Pai Ahitapasoni Kadhiti, hit dewoonia vadhavitt, Nahi ga shrutiparauti mauli jaga
  (It means vedas or Shruti is like mother who makes us to turn back from self-interest [*hitahe*], and turn towards benefit.)

The priests specializing in chanting of hymns had to be specially trained. The test of Samveda is tailored to the learning of melodies. Education in music, musical instruments was known to and taught by Rishis. The education in Vedic period involved auxiliary sciences such as Siksha, Kalpa, Vyakarana and so on. By Sutra Age (c.400-200 BC) a number of independent and allied sciences like Philosophy, Yoga; Grammar, were developed. After 1000 BC, Vedas and Vedangas were offered as courses in Vedic schools to which students were admitted at the age of 12, and such students spent 12 years of their lives at Vedic schools. The students spent their time in studying vedas, living self-controlled lives, and serving their Gurus in lieu of free board and lodging. These students were known as "Vratacharis" or "Brahmacharies". The students at the Vedic schools had to undergo physical and spiritual disciplines, had to worship Agni twice a day; they had to beg alms. Women were free to be brahmacharies. The life at schools required to do physical labour (Shrama), and to practise self-restraint.

In ancient India, curriculum used to be quite vast and all four vedas had to be learnt by heart. The students had to study Upanishads and Puranas also. During part of Vedic period, the education which was imparted was known as "Brahmani education". This "Brahmani Education" had given birth to a civilization. Till India came under the influence of Buddhist education, the Brahmani education continued to enlighten people's life. There are some special things or special features of Vedic education which are given below:

(1) Education always aimed at total development of the man. The Brahmani education system was useful for preparing people for Brahmacharya, Grihsthashram, Vanprasthashram, and Sanyasashram. Education was not bookish; it was based on practical knowledge and experiments, and experiences.

(2) Education was never thrust on children. The capacity and taste of students were taken into account.

(3) There was no difference in male and female; both were eligible for education.

(4) To obtain Brahmdyan, one needed to have humility, devotion towards teachers, and restraint on body-organs.

(5) Education was based on the knowledge of psychology.

(6) The most of the education used to be given at Gurukul, Gurugrih, and Ashram.

(7) Environment use to be the most important subject in Vedic education.

(8) The education in Vedic days was "dharmadharit"; it means education in Vedic period was founded on "Dharma".

(9) The attitude of students towards their teachers was one of humility, love, faith. The students used to be engrossed in serving the teacher, i.e., rendering "Guru-Seva". Teacher-student relations were like father-son. The students from wealthy families, even Kings, Emperor families had to be engaged in day-to-day chores, and to bring "Bhiksha".

(10) The period of study used to be of 10 to 12 years. The system of Gurukul used to be free of any charges; and it was free (mukta) from any external authority, pressure, power-exertion. The Vedic education was not affected by political changes.

(11) In Vedic age, the arrangements for education were made such that both the spiritual and worldly lives would be helped. There were intimate (very close) relations between teachers and students. There was respect, and warm and cordial relationship between them.

(12) The fundamental aim of education was to keep body, mind, and speech under control (self-control), and to be free from three debts namely, Rishiruna, Devruna, and pitruruna.

Uttar Vedic period (UVP) is taken to be 1000 BC to 200 BC. In this age Upanishads, Brahmanyak, Aaranyak were all composed.

The major aims of education were:

(1) All-round development of the individual,
(2) To build character,
(3) Development of individual personality,
(4) Develop individuality,
(5) To develop civic sense, social responsibility,
(6) Increase in religiosity,
(7) To promote social development,
(8) To work at socially useful body,
(9) Devotion to God.

In ancient period also, India was an agricultural country and, therefore, agriculture, forest produce, animal husbandry were the subjects taught. In educational method, hearing, listening, constant thinking or contemplation (*manan*), reflecting (*chintan*), experimentation and practical aspects were required. The tradition of teachers (*Guru prampara*) had the greatest importance, and status. It is due to this "parampara" that vedas are alive even today. Ancient Indian education had developed or progressed due to spirituality, restraint on our mind-stuff and thought-waves (*chitt-Vritti Nirodh*).

The Vedic scholars used to offer variety of courses to meet the demands of the time. The subjects of "the plough and the loom" were not taught in early Vedic period. Ancient India's Uttar-vedic times were the Golden period of Indian education.

During the Upanishadic period, the Rigvedic system of education continued to work. The importance of this method was its requirement to serve the Guru and his family, and manual labour helped in developing mental and moral qualities, and equipped him to receive the highest level of education and highest knowledge. This system of education was equally demanding from the teachers also. The teacher was to possess the highest moral and spiritual qualifications. The teachers were to illuminate the inner beings of his pupils with his own spiritual attainment.

In the days of Vedas, the teachers were mostly Brahmins, and they used to be from priestly classes.

During the period of 400 BC to 200 BC, the intense activities, intense work of compilation, codification, and simplification of the existing religious scriptures took place in India. In those years, Brahmanism was challenged by Buddhism. The struggle for self-assertion, self-preservation took place because Brahmanism was contested, challenged by Buddhism; it was a struggle for survival. The new literary activity which emerged to meet the challenge of Buddhism is known as sutra-age. Sutra means aphorism or short sayings. *Sutrayug* is generally taken to begin with the composition of the standard Sanskrit Grammar by Panini, and the commentary by Patanjali. During this period of 200 years, the Brahminical education system more or less continued as per the old system. In Sutra age, the student had to spend 12 years at the place of his teacher or Guru. The first school term was devised to clean the hair, and to bully the students. The education needed a study of all vedas required 48 years of student's life. The completion of education required 12 years of stay at "Gurugriha".

The Vedic or Rigvedic period has been the most enlightening, redeeming period in human history. The wisdom it purveyed was simply fantastic. This period has been defined variously by different people. One estimate puts it to be 20,000 years. Some people argue that it has been at least 10,000 years old.

India had the most outstanding civilization which was the product of religious teachings by Hindu, Buddhist, Jains, etc. religions. India had a few names which reflected the religious harmony and peace. Bharat, Bharat varsha, Jambudvipa, Brahmrshidesh, or Berahmavarta, Aryavartas, and Hindustan. The main aim of education in ancient era was to achieve emancipation, liberation or "Moksha".

Generally, the student did not have to pay fees; they were self-reliant or self-dependent. If necessary, vidyarthi used to ask for alms to meet the expenses. The education was primarily oral, Gurukul was a very important institution; the students had to observe Brahmacharya.

The important aspect of ancient education was the "Varna vyavastha" which had been born in Vedic period. It was not run on hereditary principle; it was founded on the theory of division of labour; obtaining knowledge was not confined up to any "Varna", its working was based on the strength, capacity, qualifications, and skill formation of the individuals. In Rigvedic period, both practical (vyavaharic) and spiritual education was imparted. For the common man, the arrangements were made to teach material education. The education in ancient time covered funeral pyres.

The ancient Indian system of education has been known as Vedic or Brahmnic education system. Some people think that the age or period of Vedic system of education is from eternity to 500 AD. This period was divided in three segments: (a) Rigvedic period—which is from eternity to 1000 BC; (b) The Vedic period—from 1000 BC to 200 BC, this has been also known as Upanishadic period; (c) Sutra period—200 BC to 500 AD.

As it has been mentioned earlier, the ancient Indian system of education used to work well; it exerted for the total development of the individual. It used to save the students from any attraction or desires which may waylay the individual. Devotion or Bhakti or worship of God, faith in "Dharma", character building, development of personality, fulfilling the social and civil responsibilities, the protection of National Culture were all taught in vedic education. To put it differently, ancient education had the following aims:

(i) To develop spirituality, "dharmikari" and faith, worship in God.
(ii) To develop ethical values and bring about character building.
(iii) To develop the personality of individual, and to develop courage, self-confidence, self-respect of the individual.
(iv) To develop the social values, to protect and propagate culture, and in order to do so, impart education of various sciences, trades, industry. Every student was taught the hereditary trade, hereditary work. Every family used to teach its trade to their descendants.

Education in India in the Era of Buddha

In 5th and 6th centuries BC Siddhartha, the Gautam Buddha, and Mahavir Jain laid the foundation of heterodox belief system in education. The monks of Jainism and Buddhism taught to the initiated. The whole educational work took place in Viharas, Sanghas, and monasteries.

In the period of Buddhism, "Vihar" or "Matha" were the major centres of education or learning. One cannot separate "Sanghas" from Buddhist education. "Pravraja" used to be the first ritual of

Buddhist system of education. After "pravraja" the student (*Shraman*) used to enter the "Mathas". For inclusion in "Mathas", the student had to loudly say, "Buddham Sharanam Gacchhami", "Sangham Sharanam Gacchhami", "Dhammam Sharanam Gacchhami". There was no bar in respect of caste on the entry into "Mathas". Any one of the age of eight years or more can enter the "Mathas". In Budhism, the systems of "Gurukul" or "Ashram" did not exist.

Buddhist system of education began with the destruction of home life, it superceded the home. The "Viharas" were specialized in only spiritual and religious training and taught no other subject. This was unlike Vedic system. Viharas did not have to struggle for existence, and they lived in charity. Many people joined Viharas to solve their problem of existence or survival.

The Buddhist system of learning was based on religious scriptures of Budhism, just as Brahmnical system of learning was based on Vedic scriptures. One may draw conclusion here that for a healthy, emancipatory system of education, we need religion, scriptures, and spirituality. The efforts to create educational system in a secular mode would not yield desired results. The nucleus of Buddhist system of education was "the order of monks", Shramanas, and Bhikus. The "Order of Monks" was kept open to all castes although in the beginning primarily Brahmanas and Kshtriyas had become the members of Order. Ultimately, women also were permitted to join the Order.

Budhism gave an impetus to the use and study of the local dialects and vernaculars. Bhikus were extended all facilities for training and practice in the handicrafts such as spinning, weaving, and stitching. The emphasis was given on debates and discussions such that Bhikus got training for spreading the philosophy of Budhism.

Sidhartha Gautam progenited a system of education which was similar, in some respects, and dissimilar in some other respects. Here one may recall a view that Budhism or Baudha dharma is not a new dharma; it is only a reflection of Hindu Dharma. It arose because Hindu or vaidic Vedic dharma got corrupted at some time. Budhist system of education is an image of Vedic system.

In the era of Buddha, the primary or elementary education used to begin from the age of seven years. At the elementary stage itself the students were taught *"Shabda vidya"*, *"Shilpa vidya"*,

"Chikitsa vidya", *"Hetu vidya"* and *"Spiritual vidya"*. In Budhist mathas, religions, worldly philosophy, and practical knowledge used to be imparted. Mechanism of education and study was Pali language. After ending or finishing the study of five vidyas mentioned above, the students used to learn Grammar, religion, jyotish, philosophy, etc. and this used to complete the general or ordinary, common education. Since the study (Adhyan) of these subjects was taught well, there was a flow of students from abroad to India. India had a high place in the international arrangements. Budhism had revolutionized the field of education.

However, with the passage of time, there was a revival of Vedic religion and a decline of Budhism. In any case, special features and principles of Buddhism were as follows:

(1) Except *"Chandalas"*, everybody had a right to education.
(2) The beginning of study used to be eight years of age, and the total period of study used to be 22 years.
(3) The students had to live under a very strict discipline.
(4) The students had to beg for alms.
(5) In Curriculum, different religions, philosophies, logic, and spirituality were included for study and teachings.
(6) Medium of education was the existing languages.
(7) While Buddhist religion depended on alms in a big way, Vedic religion allowed begging to a very limited extent.
(8) Both Buddhist and Vedic religions believed in simplicity.
(9) Both believed in the value of non-violence.
(10) Both believed in the physical cleanliness and sacredness.
(11) Vedic system of education was house or home or family-centered, while Budhist system of education was sangh-centric.
(12) The educational institutions could be individualistic in Vedic system but such individualistic institutions were not encouraged in Budhist religion.
(13) In Vedic education, only the Brahmins could be teachers. But this was only in the beginning. Later on, it was accepted that anybody could become teacher like what was the practice in Budhism.
(14) The medium of education was Sanskrit in Vedic religion, while it was Pali under Budhism.

Islamic Education

The Muslim invaders had invaded India, and they had arrived in India in the 8th century itself. The Muslim age in Bharat was during 1206 to 1858 years. It means that Muslim age in India was of the order of 650 years. In this age, many changes in education took place. From 13th century AD to 18th century AD, the invaders had a great influence on the education in India. From 13th century to 18th century AD some Sultans had set up madarsas, but the rulers generally did not show much concern for the education of the common people.

There were two parts of Islamic education. In the beginning, the education activity used to take place in maktaba. The second part which was related to the higher level of education used to be given in Madarsas. Islamic education had certain specific features:

(1) This education was practical, it had very close connection with life.

(2) There used to be harmony between primary-level and secondary-level education. To repeat, in Islamic educational era while maktaba was for primary education, higher level education was imparted in madarsas. Some madarsas had assumed the nature and character of the universities. The students used to enter madrasa after completing primary level studies. Very erudite persons used to live in madrasa which used to receive funds from the rulers, so that they should not suffer from financial difficulties. This means that education was financially independent or education was self-relief only in the case of Vedic education, in other cases, education was not required to be self-sufficient.

The curriculum in madarsas was of two types, namely Religious and Worldly. Students used to spend 10-12 years at madarsas. The medium of education used to be Arabic. The subjects taught and learned were quite varied. They were: grammar, prose writings, poetry, logic, law, etc. Maktab and madarsas were the places where Koran, and other Muslim religious books were taught.

One very great thing which happened during Muslim era was that it was during this period that Hindus started learning Farsi, and Muslims started learning Sanskrit.

Out of this interaction was born the new language which came to be known, as "Urdu". Islamic education had the following aims:

(a) To spread or to distribute knowledge-light (dnyan Prakash) among all the Muslims. Every true muselman must try to obtain knowledge.
(b) To propagate, to spread the religion of Muslims.
(c) To get, to receive salary, money, wealth.
(d) To develop the personality of every individual; to work for material progress, intellectual development, and moral/ethical elevation or upliftment.

In the medieval and early modern periods, the Muslim educational models were brought to India. Muslim rulers promoted urban education, they found privacy schools. From the beginning of the Mugal period, they found primary schools around 1000 BC.

IV. Indian Education in Post-Islamic Period

This period can be said to cover modern period, or pre-Independence and post-Independence period, or British Raj period (Company Sarkar and King's Rule).

In order to complete the picture of the Indian education, let us present here the account of the major happenings in Indian education during the modern era comprising 1700 to 1947 AD. We present briefly the account of the major developments, events, incidents, occurrences during the modern era which has been mostly put at 1700 to 1947 AD. During this period, long-drawn struggle for political independence was waged by the Indian people. India became a free nation on August 15, 1947 as a result of the fight with the Britishers.

One of the first important things that took place, after India became a sovereign Nation, was to give to themselves the Constitution of India in 1950 (January 26, 1950). This Constitution directed the nation that by the end of 10 years, every child would have received education. The Government miserably failed to achieve this target. The response of the Government to this failure was to put the target in the mandatory part of the Constitution and making it a fundamental right of the children. This is very queer, and no one would be enthused by such dances of paper tigers.

Even then, we can give solace to ourselves because some good things also have happened in the educational sector in India in the recent past. For example, almost in all the areas, there has been a significant increase in all types and all levels of educational institutions, and the number of students. The Government appointed many committees and commissions which have suggested policies for tackling the problems in the educational sector. Unfortunately, the policy of "reforms by committees" has failed completely. The education in India has regressed in terms of quality. Education in India is characterized by a very high level of indiscipline.

The beginning of modern education in India was made through commercial and religious goals. The "Company Sarkar" had kept its educational activities limited initially. That activity was confined to serving the requirements of British and other European children. But slowly, the East India Company (EIC) realized that educational policy should be to revamp the education such that the interests of both Indian and foreign children would be taken care of. As a result, from 1765 many institutions were opened up. The period had 7-year education. In 1791 Banaras Sanskrit College was established. Similarly, Madarsas were set up in Calcutta. The British policy underlying these changes was called orientalist policy. This policy had maintained religious neutrality so that Indian people were not disturbed or agitated.

From pre-independence to post-independence years, persons like Mahatma Phule, Karve, and others had carried out educational reforms. This work to increase the quantity and raise the quality of education should not be overlooked. After Independence, particularly after 1990, the education in India suffered from degradation. The policy of liberalization, deregulation, globalization has disoriented the Indian education. There has been increase in corruption and falsity.

It appears that in the early years of Nineteenth Century another debate took place which was about the status of Sanskrit language. In this context, the then Viceroy, Lord Ripen constituted a committee namely, Hunter Commission, in 1881. This body studied, found and observed the following:

(i) The present state and development of primary education need to be paid more attention.

(ii) The newer and newer person should be informed who would help those lagging behind.
(iii) What is the role of Missionary schools in India?
(iv) The Government policy should pay attention to individuals.
(v) Financial help to be rendered.

This work was followed up by appointing various committees, viz. Indian University Education Commission (1902) which made recommendations regarding various aspects of the functioning of universities. In 1904, the Viceroy released the proposal on education. One of the main drawbacks of the Indian University education system was that it overstressed the goal of jobs creation. It was found that it had become excessively more job-oriented and examination-oriented. Further, too much stress was given on memory and not intellect. In 1904, Gokhale put forth a proposal which emphasized that impetus needs to be given to the primary education. Thus, some efforts (public and private) were made to strengthen Indian education.

Although on the face of it, it appeared that foreign rulers were genuinely interested in Indian public welfare. The real aim of their education policy was to train peons, clerks, translators to successfully run the Raj. They made English as the medium of education and neglected the vernaculars. They introduced policies, including educational policy, to serve the British Raj.

In December 1947 Indian Educational Conference took place and Indian Government Constituted Radhakrishnan Committee to suggest improvement in University education.

In the first part of 19th century (around 1813) a few important issues were debated in India. First, should there be free entry? Second, should we allow the people to propagate religion in India or not? Third, whose responsibility is it to educate the people? After a long and hot debate, it was decided that those who want to engage in "spreading education" and "spreading religion" should be given all facilities as per law. It was also decided that the responsibility of educating those living in India must be taken up by EIC. It was also debated that as to what way, or what method should be used to spread education free of cost. Many people were in favour of "Shravana" "theorem". According to this method, English education should be given to a few people through the medium of English language. These few people who are educated through English medium will then teach common people through their own country language. Thus, it was Britisher's plan that educational organization, educational structure should be such that it automatically create an unequal social order. Ironically, this "Nisyana theory" was rejected by the overwhelming majority in the British times, but it came to be widely accepted and implemented by Indians later on.

We end this discussion on Indian education by mentioning two or three policy measures announced by the Government during the post-Independence period. First, the Constitution was amended to provide free and compulsory education to all.

Second, education for all, "Sarva Shiksha Abhiyan" was launched in 1995 to ensure that every one in India gets education. Third, Mid-day meals scheme was introduced so that school-going children do not remain absent from schools, and those children do not suffer from malnutrition. Four, the Governments would set up Navodaya Vidyalayas from 1990. We will return to this subject and discuss at some length the state of education in India on the eve of the current year 2015.

4

Modern Indian Educational System

This chapter briefly discusses the Indian and world contemporary Educational System. The salient features, problems, faults, shortcomings, drawbacks, inadequacies i.e. the state of world educational system at present are to be adumbrated in this chapter.

(1) Table 1 shows that the number of recognized educational institutions has increased significantly during 1951 to 2006. A sizeable increase in the number of teachers has taken place. A significant increase in the enrolment at all levels, and a decline in dropout rate has occurred. The improvement in terms of education of females, caste persons has taken place. An increase in literacy levels or literacy rate has also taken place. The expenditure on education has also occurred.

(2) It has been pointed out that financial and other resources are not available in adequate measure; and they have been unduly fluctuating. It has been argued that this has adversely affected the quality, excellence in education. There has also been an issue of who should give the finance? Some people have argued that funds for education should of course be provided by the State through budgets. Persons like Gandhi-Vinoba have argued that if we are frugal, not much money is required. Moreover, education sector ought to be self-reliant.

(3) The Constitutional resolve, provision, amendment to promote, provide free and compulsory education to all

children of school-going age is yet to be fulfilled, honoured; this objective has remained a non-starter.

(4) The homogeneous relationship between education and industry has still not taken place.

(5) IES has been providing or trading degrees by collecting fees like tin-pot shops. IES has been commercialized unprecedentally.

(6) IES has been vulnerable to all kinds of risks. The colleges, universities have become a mere examination bodies, and even that task is riddled with so many drawbacks, faults such as question paper leakages. Educational institutions have become examination-centric.

(7) To be educated only for job or employment is to lower or trivialize the purpose of life of human being (his destiny) vis-à-vis birds and animals. It is an alarming development that question papers, certificates, degrees, etc. are now available on city footpaths.

(8) There has been a mushroom growth of shady, unrecognized, etc. educational institutions which are the private empires of education emperors (shikshan samrat).

(9) IES is the second name of low or bad quality, total irrelevance, bookish knowledge or low knowledge, or little knowledge or no knowledge?

(10) The excellence in education or competition success is measured by the fatness of pay-packages (where one thousand means one K in the lingo that is getting developed). It is a sad thing that the vulture-culture or corporates has absorbed, sponge-like, the Principals, Directors, and Faculty in its regime. Education is meant to establish culture of non-violence and peace. Education has achieved exactly its opposite because of the rule of money and power as dominant motivation.

(11) The quality of teachers and teaching environment are poor. The education sector is somehow carrying its task with inadequate school space (buildings, laboratories, blackboards, and toilets, etc.). The habit of giving lip service, and putting the tasks in "mission mode" have contributed to the failure.

(12) The crucial value of "autonomy" is very often seriously, dangerously comprised. The policies of the Government

to function through Ordinance Raj and "Schemes Raj" also contributed to failures. There are too many welfare schemes which have to be implemented by the school staff including teachers. Are the schools for providing food or knowledge? Is the Nation for Roti or *Vidya*? The Government policy compromising the motto, "Matru Hasten bhojanam".

(13) Is IES elitist? Is it equitous? Is it equal opportunity giver? Does it promote social justice? The replies to such questions are a big No in every case.

(14) The pattern of allocation of budgetary resources continues to be unsatisfactory. The rural-urban divide is very glaring in this respect even now.

(15) The present education policy is based on a wrong assumption that men and women are equal. In fact, women are superior to men.

(16) The IES is afflicted by many problems, faults, and so on.

(17) The educational system in India has, inter alia, three defects.

- English education was given. There was no integration between work and standard of living.
- Education ought to be made independent of the Government proceeds.
- Educational activities should be free from Government interference.

(18) Normally, education is said to provide solution to many problems. But instead, education itself has become a problem.

(19) Education is not related to life. Today's education has become inappropriate, irrelevant.

(20) Today's education is such that there is no Brahmavidya in it, there is no work in it. As a result, all the people are devotees of "vishaya-sukh".

(21) The young people have become enjoyment and pleasure seekers they have become slaves of "Bhoga". There is no work, labour, Udyoga in education. Consequently, hands are becoming idle. In the present system of education, intellect and body are becoming unused. Therefore, we have to change, revolutionize today's education by

bringing in Brahma *Vidya* or spirituality and work (udyoga).

(22) Indian socio-political-economic system is known as Mixed Economy (Welfare State, Democracy). The important implication of adopting this model has been that the governance, functioning, planning, policy-making are divided into public (State, Government) sector and private sector. Education also is subject to such a division or marking. The planning, development, policies, initiatives, innovations, administration, management, execution, etc. are done by following a Public-Private-Partnership (PPP) approach. In respect of education, there is neither a total socialization, nationalization nor a complete laissez-faire, free market or marketization. The debate on public vs. private sectors in education is also the debate on centralization vs. decentralization. The desirable goal in this context should be maximum decentralization with emphasis on greater role for local bodies.

(23) All present schools are set up and managed by Central and State Governments, local bodies (district boards, municipalities, rich families, family trusts, churches and temples, and philanthropy, religious organizations (viz. Arya Samaj, Chinmaya Mission), registered Trust bodies and philanthropy. The private schools are divided into two parts: Aided and Unaided.

(24) Indian Educational System is ancient and it has been blessed and shaped by the active participation and blessings of a galaxy of sages, munis, rishis, yogis and so on. Apart from the seers of Rigveda, Patanjali, Buddha, Mahavir Jain, enlightened people have created heterodox belief systems of education.

(25) It has been pointed out that from Vedic age downwards, the central conception of education of the Indians has been that it is the source of illumination. The man has really three eyes, the third eye being that of knowledge. It is also called inner eye (Antachakshu) which gives man insight into all affairs.

India was the only country where University education almost on modern type existed as early as 800 BC or earlier. The learning and culture of ancient India was chiefly the point of her hermitages in the solitude of the forests. It was not of the cities or towns. Indian civilization has, therefore, been called as "Aranyak" culture.

(26) Gandhi-Vinoba can be said to be the earliest advocates of "deschooling". Both of them did not attend school. More significantly, they asked children to leave schools.

(27) Our present system of education is so bad that it should be destroyed by burning at the earliest. In fact, it is not good enough even for burning. It is eating away the heart of India. All the students community should demand in one voice that this system be burned at once.

(28) Shruti, Smriri, Kriti, Yoga, *Vidya* sah yoga constitute ancient Indian science of education.

(29) The words one comes across while studying New Education are: Nai Talim; New Education, Basic Education, Buniyadi, Pre-basic, Uttar Buniyadi, Senior basic, Post-basic, Nitya Nai Talim.

(30) Undue extent of worry about mobilizing funds and other requirements.

(31) The educational sector is suffering from the apathy of parents and students.

(32) There is a widespread collusion and corruption in the educational sector.

(33) The falling quality/standards is resulting in impoverishment of the IES.

(34) The greed for money-making rule is the roost in educational sector.

(35) The mother tongue has been treated in unjust and injurious manner by not giving it the status of medium of education.

(36) The privatization of education has harmed this vital sector of the economy.

(37) The word 'excellence in education' has become trivialized, divisive, etc. instead of becoming enriched over the years.

(38) The technology fetish has resulted in contradictory, paradoxical policies. The schools now even lack enough blackboards, classrooms.

(39) The number and diversity of educational institutions and abodes of deities or temples (devasthanams) have grown phenomenally but spirituality and the number of well-educated people has highly declined over the years. The

spread of education has not resulted in the spread of "sushikshata". The quantitative and qualitative dimensions of education have not kept pace with each other.

(40) There has been a flood-like increase in the state intervention in the working of education. The autonomy of institutions has been reduced.

(41) There has been a really harmful entry of party-politics, and election politics in the working of IES.

(42) As educational sector has been unproductive, the institutions do not have enough resources.

(43) There has been an increase in violence in schools and other educational institutes.

(44) Today, the teachers are more interested in power (*adhikar*) than in learning (*adhyan*) and teaching (*adhyapan*).

(45) The modern civilization is transforming everything into commerce, business, industry, profit-making enterprise. Like agriculture, culture, entertainment, education has become an industry and the efforts are directed to make it a lucrative profitable industry. The latest idea is to convert Universities into corporate bodies.

(46) The teaching institutions have become teaching, training shops, concerns, enterprises, or factories. We have heard of education-samrats like sugar-samrats in Maharashtra. Education has become a closely-held/family/single politician and the private proprietorship business.

(47) The examination syndrome, which begins at the age of about 2.5 years, results in children developing anxiety and a negative attitude to education.

(48) The basic assumptions, premises of the present education are faulty. It assumes that man by nature is weak, immoral, wicked and animal like and it is the task of education to make him man. It also presumes that life essentially involves competition, conflicts. These features/ills are universal.

(49) There has been a lop-sided growth of technical and management education at the cost of teaching of languages, humanities, certain social sciences, and the classics. The phenomenal mushrooming of the engineering and management colleges/institutions shows this.

(50) The education has become examination-oriented and the examination system has become riddled with many vices.

The instances of children committing suicides due to examination-pressure are increasing. It appears that we are examining and educating children to death.

(51) The majority of students who emerge from our educational system are afflicted by the malady called tunnel-vision i.e. an ability to parrot institutionalization of everything rather than non-professional ministration of the neighbour.

(52) Although we are very enamoured by everything American, and the maximum of our brain-drain is to America, many perceptive Americans and others are totally disillusioned with the American system of education.

(53) Alexander Astin has argued that something is terribly wrong with the state of American democracy, and the higher education may have played a part in creating this crisis in American democracy. The American educational system has failed to promote "good citizenship" among the people.

(54) It is interesting to note that the East-West divide does not exist in the field of education. As Ivan Illich has said, "other basic institutions—family, party, press, church—might differ from country to country, but not the schools. They are not dependent on ideology; they are basically alike in fascist, democratic, socialist countries. They are alike in structure, purpose, hidden curriculum which is directed to shape the consumer.

(55) Many people have complained that the American children have become increasingly illiterate in their culture, history, mathematics.

(56) In late 1960s, the Carnegie Commission in USA had described the American Education as follows: "In the schools, the registered students submit to certified teachers in order to obtain certificates of their own. Both are frustrated and both blame insufficient resources—money, time, infrastructure—for their mutual frustration."

(57) Einstein has once said that "degree courses are at best incomplete and at worst useless."

(58) Theodore Rozak has said that education in America and everywhere is nothing but the machine tooling of young

minds to serve the baroque bureaucracies in the Government, corporations, universities, armies, etc.

According to Gandhi-Vinoba's perception and viewpoint, the fault of today's IES, is that it separates knowledge (Vidya) and work (Karma) from each other. Today, education means read and write and sit in the chair and give orders. The work (Karma) is regarded unnecessary while getting knowledge (vidya). The students at present feel ashamed of work or physical labour. It is very dangerous to separate body (*deha*) from intellect (*buddhi*). The healthy situation would be one in which a learned, erudite person is dutiful, devoted to duty (*karmanishta*) also. In true education, knowledge and (Physical) work or *Vidya* and (Physical) labour should join with each other. In today's education, one gets neither practical knowledge nor spiritual knowledge. Today's education has no contact with reality. Today's educated person does not understand, he is unaware of mystic experiences.

Today's education is examination and job centered. The student is no longer a student or Vidyarthi, he has become mere examinee. The aim of education is to equip the student to obtain knowledge on his own or independently. What is supplied today is not knowledge but some information.

In Vinoba's words, 'I am totally dissatisfied with today's education. When I was in a college, I used to feel that every moment of my life is being wasted. Today's education is most worthless (raddi). The schools are lifeless; they make you literate, but they do not give knowledge that is useful for life. Today's education is comfort-seeking or easy-going. We have committed all the mistakes which were possible to commit about education.'

In today's education, *vidyalayas* (educational institutions) have come to mean the places from which knowledge has disappeared.

In *Hind-Swaraj*, and in his book, *Towards New Education*, Gandhiji has explained, inter alia, the inadequacies of the prevailing education. As soon as we say education, the majority of people would say that education means teaching, reading, writing, and arithmetic. This is known as primary education or knowledge of letters. It is known as liberal education. Now, this education does not really benefit a peasant or anybody else; it does not make any one happy. The fault of present kind of education is that it emphasizes and tries to provide this faulty type of education.

The teaching of subjects like Geography, Astronomy, Algebra also do not help anyone to control our senses. To elaborate, Gandhiji is not against studying sciences mentioned above; he held that they have their place in education when (after) we have controlled our senses, and put our ethics on a firm foundation. There is a difference in priorities in today's education and Gandhiji. He advised that we should not make fetish, as we are doing today, of teaching letters, etc. Gandhiji wanted character-building, control of senses, ethical and moral upliftment to precede learning letters and liberal education.

The IES in the words of Gandhiji was as follows: 'I have never been able to make a fetish of literary training. My experience has proved to my satisfaction that literary training by itself adds not an inch to one's moral height. I am firmly of the opinion that government schools have unmanned us, rendered us hopeless. They have filled us with discontent, and providing no remedy discontent, have made us despondent. They have made us what we were intended to become, clerks interpreters.' He had argued the prevailing education is false education, rotten education. To give millions knowledge of English was to enslave them. Mccaulay's scheme of education which we are implementing today has enslaved us. According to Gandhi-Vinoba, present education in India is rotten and "raddi" (useless, worthless).

The world-wide assessment of recent major trends and changes in education revealed that there was an emerging crisis in world education. What has happened to the educational crisis in the world since 1960s? Where does it stand now? What are the most critical common issues world education is facing today.

American education is in a state of present increasing crisis and confusion. These have grown progressively worse over the years. The various reasons for this has been: (a) the rapid pace of technology and industrialism, and (b) the inability of the schools to adapt themselves to these alterations in the society. The schools are in trouble.

Thus, education abroad at present is in the sick, pathological condition or in an extremely sorry state of affairs. Many scholars in India argue that if we want to improve, to change for the better, to reform, education in India, we will have to learn from the experience of other countries. This is a hopeless path doomed to fail because certain scholars, educationists abroad tell us that the state of education in countries like the UK, the USA, France is equally bad.

Alvin Toffler in his book *Future Shock* has this to say about Western education. 'What possess for education today, even in our "best" schools and colleges, is a hopeless anachronism.' The Indian sub-system of education is dangerously mal-functioning. The parents view education to fit their children for life in future. The teachers warn that lack of education will cripple the child's chances in the world of tomorrow. Everybody exhort all young people to stay in schools, insisting that now, as never before, one's future is almost wholly dependent upon education. But in reality, as Toffler went on to state that 'schools face backward in the direction of a dying system, rather than forward toward a developing system'. To help avert the future shock we must create super industrial education system.

The present world educational system in the view of Carnegie Commission, is the product of industrialization and the values of modern civilization. As referred to above, in present schools, registered students submit to certified teachers for obtaining certificates. Both students and teachers are frustrated, and both blame insufficient resources for their mutual frustration in the USA.

The great scientist Albert Einstein has also said that degree courses are at best incomplete and at worst useless. The illiteracy of American students in Maths, History, Culture and Literature is surprising.

In the recent past, reforms or even revolution in IES has received considerable attention in the world. Two approaches are usually talked of in this context: Indian approach and the Western approach. While the latter is more technology-driven, the former is deeper and holistic. The evolution of IES has been, unfortunately, imitative. The industrialization, commercialization philosophy has influenced strongly the Indian evolution as well as Western evolution. The growth of educational systems in both the East and the West has been similar. This system has not served even the East as well as the West. The system has not served well because the underlying approach has been expedient, inefficient, expensive and bureaucratic. The IES and the Western education system (WES) have failed.

The educational institutions have become market-places and

the centres of politics. Someone has made a very observant remark that if one wants to see real politics, one should go to colleges, and universities. There has been a collusion between the educationists and politicians. The issue of reservations has come in the way of rebuilding or reconstructing the Nation.

The education is becoming increasingly more costly which is making it more exclusive rather than inclusive. The private sector education is making education unnecessarily competitive, more and more costly.

At present, the conditions of the teachers at all levels are pathetic indeed. They are not paid adequate salaries; salaries are not paid regularly either, they are paid with long delays; the new categories like "education sevaks" have been created and they are paid pittance as salaries; very often candidates aspiring for the jobs are required to donate a year's salary or two year's salary in advance for getting the job as teachers. They have to perform all kinds of jobs in the elections processes which have tended to multiply over the period of time.

The educationists like Bloom, Hirsch from the USA have emphasized that education must enable us to recover, to reassert what has been nearly lost namely, great moral truths upon which the civilization rests. The education is not merely about facts, it is about truth and the state of our soul. Another vice of the American educational system is very high costs. Even in America, generally students are apathetic, bored, they are treated as a COS in the machine. The education needs to become deeply personalized, if we want to identify and build on a child's strength etc.

Table 1: Number of Recognised Educational Institutions in India, 1981-2006

Year	Primary	Upper primary	Higher	Colleges for general edn.	Colleges for professional edn.	Universities
	(1)	(2)	(3)	(4)	(5)	(6)
1950-51	209671	13596	7416	370	208	27
1970-71	408378	90621	375051	2285	992	82
1990-91	560935	151456	79796	4882	986	184
2000-01	638738	206269	126047	7929	2223	254
2005-06	771082	288199	154032	11549	4992	350

Note: Column 4 includes High / Higher / Secondary / inter / preliminary / Junior college.

Source: RBI, *Handbook of Statistics on The Indian Economy*, 2007-08, p. 281.

Table 2: Public Expenditure on Education in India during Plan Periods (Absolute Figures in Rs. Crores (1951-2012)

Period	*Total expenditure*	*Expenditure on edn. (% to total)*	*Expenditure on elementary edn.*	*Expenditure on secondary edn. (% to total)*	*Expenditure on higher edn. (% to total)*
	(1)	(2)	(3)	(4)	(5)
1951-56	1960	7.6	56	13	31
1956-61	4672	5.85	35	29	46
1961-66	8576	6.86	34	18	48
1966-69	6625	4.63	24	16	60
1969-74	15779	4.91	30	18	52
1979-80	39426	4.34	35	17	48
1980-85	12176	2.16	–	–	–
1985-90	110467	2.69	30	25	45
1990-92	221435	3.47	34	22	44
1992-97	123120	3.99	37	22	41
1997-02	485457	4.45	47	18	35
2002-07	813997	6.12	66	11	23
2007-12	1618460	6.26	66	10	24
	3644718	9.53	50	20	30

Source: Kumar Ganesh, Growth and Development of Education in India, since 1951-52, *Political Economy Journal of India,* January 1, 2011.

Table 3: Public Expenditure on Education in India in Relation to GDP

Period	*EE as % of GDP*	*Number of Universities*
	(1)	(2)
1951-52	0.64	27
1961-62	1.52	45
1971-72	2.25	82
1981-82	2.83	110
1991-92	3.80	184
2001-02	3.80	272
2005-06	3.46	350

Note: Figures in column 2 are Universities, Deemed Universities and Institutes of National Importance.

Table 4: Enrolment of all Categories of Students in India, 1950-51 to 2005-2006 (Figures in Millions)

Period	*Preliminary (I-V) and Upper Primary (VI-VIII)*			*Secondary and Senior Secondary (IX-XVII)*			*Higher Education*		
	Boys	*Girls*	*Total*	*Boys*	*Girls*	*Total*	*Boys*	*Girls*	*Total*
1950-51	13.8	5.4	19.2	2.6	0.5	3.1	1.3	0.2	1.5
1960-61	23.6	11.4	35.0	5.1	1.6	6.7	2.7	0.7	3.4
1970-71	35.7	21.3	57.0	9.4	3.9	13.3	5.7	1.9	7.6
1980-81	45.3	28.5	73.8	13.9	6.8	20.1	7.6	3.4	11.0
1990-91	57.0	40.4	97.4	21.5	17.5	34.0	12.8	6.3	19.1
2001-02	63.6	50.3	113.9	26.1	18.7	42.8	18.4	10.7	30.5
2004-05	69.7	61.1	130.8	25.5	22.7	51.2	22.3	16.1	38.4

Source: As for Table 2.

Table 5: Literacy Rate in India (in %)

Period	*Rural*			*Urban*			*All-India*		
	M	*F*	*T*	*M*	*F*	*T*	*M*	*F*	*T*
1951	19.12	4.87	12.10	45.6	22.93	34.59	27.60	8.96	18.30
1961	34.30	10.10	22.50	66.0	40.60	54.40	40.40	15.35	28.30
1971	48.60	15.50	27.90	69.60	48.80	60.20	45.96	21.97	34.55
1981	49.60	21.70	36.00	76.70	56.80	67.30	56.38	29.76	43.57
1991	57.90	30.60	44.70	81.10	64.0	73.10	64.13	39.29	52.21
2001	71.40	71.40	59.40	86.10	73.20	80.30	75.85	54.16	65.38

Notes: M = Males, F = Females, T = All persons.
Source: As for Table 2.

5

Lessons from Experiments and Experiences in Education by Gandhi-Vinoba in South Africa and India

The views and philosophy of Gandhi-Vinoba are the result of their experiments and their studies (ancient as well as modern).

People were drawn, attracted towards Gandhi as the "Patanga" is attracted to the burning lamp. He had an inexplicable hold on the people. The ability of Gandhi to successfully effect "loksangraha" was unsurpassable and inexplicable. This made him suggest that we should be able to attract all children towards ourselves, and we should treat these children as our own children. They are neither good nor bad; we should be in a position to make even small children creative. He believed that infants start learning right from the time of conception. At that point, we should teach the mother. In Mahabharata, Abhimanyu learnt the method of breaking the Chakravyuha when he was still in the womb of Subhadra, his mother. It is very interesting to know that about the education of infants, Vyas and Gandhi had similar views. As per this view, even infants have to be taught or educated; the education in infancy has two parts or components, one education of the infant through his mother (adult education), and, the education of infants. The infant education begins at the time of conception, and it continues to be imparted at the age of two or two and half years. Gandhiji had emphasized that the education of the infants should be creative and constructive, and it should never be destructive. It is thus *clear that Gandhian educational philosophy was committed to the value of non-violence from the infanthood itself.*

In infant education or in the basic education, there are no distinctions between play and education. Gandhiji has said that for him writing was a game, according to him, children should learn while playing and while earning.

It is necessary to note that Gandhiji's philosophy of education is full of interesting, deep, novel, original concepts, he has made use of psychology, children, teachers; he has created completely new characters "Mother-Teacher".

According to Gandhiji, after infant education, we have to develop a correct approach to education of boys and girls of up to ten years of age. In other words, Gandhiji has given special attention to *"early childhood education"*, education of children not exceeding 10 years of age (or education of children of 3 to 10 years of age). Education at this stage should impart knowledge of letters (i.e. the capacity to read and write). In addition, children should be taught how to use in the right way all sense organs including the mind. The child should know how to use his "five organs of action", (five *karmendriya*) and five organs of knowledge (five *dnyanedriya*).

Therefore, Gandhiji has suggested a way out of such difficulties. He said that boys and girls should be placed in surroundings, environment, atmosphere where they will get the same atmosphere as they do at home. Since of all the persons the mother is the most competent to undertake the duty of educating the children, this particularly task should be entrusted only to women. As a rule, men are far behind the women in respect of love, affection, patience. It follows that the question of the education of children cannot be solved unless efforts are made simultaneously to solve the question of women's education. Gandhiji was of the view and conviction that as long as we do not have real "mother-teachers", and "teacher-mothers", who can successfully impart true education to our children, they will remain uneducated even though they may be going to schools. On the basis of reflection and experimentation, Gandhiji came to the conclusion that primary education should be given at least for a year without the book, and even after that the use of books should be restricted to the minimum. Thus Gandhian preference was for the bookless learning.

As part of discussion on Secondary Education also, Gandhiji has given us a large number of wise things.

First of all, he emphasized that the educational systems in India should promote patriotism, it should enable India to get "Swaraj"; it should protect the freedom of nation; it should never make people to believe that what is good for the UK and other parts of Europe is good for India also. The Government education has generally been detrimental to Swaraj. A few examples supporting this approach are given below:

Foreign medium i.e. English medium has prevented the growth of our vernaculars; the foreign medium has caused brain fag, strained nerves, cramming, imitation, lack of originality. Foreign medium has made our children practically foreigners in their own land. The imposition of foreign medium, and preventing the mother tongue from becoming a medium of education has caused the greatest tragedy in India.

The nation to remain a nation must receive all instruction including the highest in its own vernaculars. Similarly, the youth in any country cannot keep or establish a living conflict with the masses unless their knowledge is received and assimilated through vernaculars. There never was a greater superstition than that a particular language was incapable of expressing abstruse or scientific ideas. A language is an exact reflection of the character and growth of its speakers. His views on higher education are briefly stated below:

(i) Gandhiji has said that he was not the enemy of Higher Education per se, but he was opposed to Higher Education as it actually was even in his time.

(ii) The State should generally not pay for higher education, except when the State has a definite use for it.

(iii) Gandhiji was opposed to any part of higher education if it was paid by the state from its general revenue.

(iv) The most of education then as now was sheer waste, it engendered mass unemployment, and it has destroyed the material, physical, mental, intellectual health.

(v) The foreign language being the medium of education has caused incalculable intellectual and moral injury to the nation.

In his assessment the higher education has only generated armies of B.As and M.As with their brains sapped with too much cramming, and minds almost paralyzed. Gandhiji wanted all this to be eliminated. The aim of University education should be coordinated and brought into line with Basic Education.

Gandhian educational thought has often been ridiculed by saying that it is utopian, irrelevant, and dated. But this is not true in actual life.

There are many cases which are a clear, direct proof of being highly and directly relevant today. For example, the current mania for establishing new universities in different places, Gandhiji has tersely pointed out that India must avoid creating many new universities. There should be a proper background for new universities. Though we are politically free, we are hardly free from subtle domination of the West. During 1990s and later, the authorities have created a large number of new IITs, IIMs, Central Universities, etc. This clustering of setting up of universities has constrained the creation of healthy, scholarly institutions. There have been grossly inadequate laboratories, and other infrastructural facilities. The same problem has come up in 1990s and 1940s.

Gandhiji learnt that spiritual training can be given in various ways: asking children to memorize and recite hymns and read to them from scriptures, and by exercising the spirit. The teacher has a very great role to play in this vital matter. The exercise of the spirit depended on the life and character and the way of living of the teacher. The teacher who is a liar cannot teach students to be truthful, a cowardly teacher cannot make valiant pupils. Gandhiji came to the conclusion, based on his experiments, that the teacher must be an eternal object-lesson to the students, who became teachers' teachers, that teachers must be good and live straight for their sakes. Gandhiji has said a wonderful thing that the increasing discipline and restraint Gandhiji imposed on himself at Tolstoy Form was mostly due to his students. After all the eternally valid utterances are:

> The child is the father of man.
> The disciple is the teacher of teacher.

What about disciplining the pupils? Gandhiji's experiments showed that he never punished his students physically; Gandhiji was always opposed to corporal punishment for his students, his children, and others. Generally, because of his own precept and practice, his students were mostly disciplined; sometimes there were cases of misconduct. Once or twice he resorted to physical punishment for the students. However, he regretted, repented that he used physical punishment or violence to correct the conduct of his students. His confession in this context is worth noting permanently. When Gandhiji punished the boy, the boy cried not because the beating was painful to him but because he realized Gandhi's pain in being driven to his violent recourse. Gandhi's further comments in this context were very instructive. He said that on the day he physically punished the student, "I exhibited not the spirit, but the brute in me. This incident set me thinking and taught me a better method of correcting students."

There is another important matter from which Gandhiji has drawn an important lesson. The question is whether we should treat students unequally, differentially for one reason or other? Gandhiji learnt a lesson at Tolstoy Farm. At this Ashram, Gandhiji's three children also studied. When it was suggested that Gandhiji should keep his boys separately, Gandhiji rejected the suggestion saying that if good children are taught together with bad ones, they will lose nothing provided experiment is conducted under the watchful care of their parents and guardians.

There is another very important issue in respect of which Gandhiji has given a very good counsel based on his experiments. The question is: should teachers go on fast as penance to improve the students in their behaviour?

Gandhiji realized that it is very difficult to bring up and educate children the right way. If one was to be a real teacher, one must touch the heart of students, one must share their joys and sorrows, and one must help them to solve their problems, and one must channel their surging aspirations suitably. Even after doing all this, some occasions would crop up when one may have to use the drastic remedy, i.e., going on a fast as penance. But it presupposes clearness of vision and spiritual fitness—where there is no true love between the teacher and the taught, where the student's delinquency has not touched the very being of the teacher, and where the pupil has no respect for the teacher, the fasting is out of place and may even be harmful. One should always remember the teacher's responsibility for the errors of his pupils.

The narrative of Gandhiji's educational experiments and the results of these experiments in India begin in the year 1915 when Gandhiji paid a visit to Shantiniketan. It is not much known that

"The Phoenix" family had been assigned separate quarters at Shantinikatan. Thus Shantinikaten can be said to be a confluence of two types of educational experiments: phoenix-developed experiments and the experiments by Gurudeva Rabindarnath Tagore.

Gandhiji initiated a "self-help" in running the kitchen or the "Kitchen Revolution". The teachers and students of phoenix, under the guidance of Gandhiji, decided to dispense with the paid cooks and to cook their food themselves. The Shantinikatan students also started a kitchen for themselves. The experiment worked well in the beginning, but it was dropped after some time. According to Gandhiji, Shantinikaten lost nothing by having conducted the experiment for a brief interval, and some of the experiences gained could not but be of help to the teachers. Gurudeva's comment was "the experiment contains the key to Swaraj".

Gandhiji's views on education have developed or evolved further in his Ashrams and his other institutions in India. It is necessary to know that the historical, evolutionary content would be transparent. Let us discuss Gandhi's views, rules, standards which constituted Gandhiji's philosophy of education.

Gandhiji argued that human being cannot overcome their weaknesses all at once.

The total period of education should be 25 years which corresponds with the period of "Brahmacharyashram", which is one of the four Ashramas into which the 100-year life span of the man or woman was divided by our forefathers or social scientists. There were other three Ashramas namely "Grihasthashram", "Vanprasthashram", and "Sanyasashrama" in that order and each having a period of 25 years. The society had enjoined on everyone to do certain duties which were Ashram-specific. It is interesting to note, however, that everyone in every Ashrama was to do education-related duties. Thus, Gandhiji had defined the period of education to be 25 years the inspiration for which was drawn from ancient social organization or social arrangements.

The total period of education was divided by Gandhiji into three stages:

First stage: 1 to 8 years.
Second stage: 9 to 16 years.
Third stage: 16 to 25 years.

The education was to be co-education. Manual training was the most important part of Gandhian educational arrangements. The education was to pay attention to the special aptitudes of the pupils. The child should first be taught to draw geometrical figures, which should be followed by learning to write the alphabets which are to be followed by learning to read. It was expected that if education precedes as per these arrangements the child will have acquired considerable knowledge by the time he became eight years old or by the end of the First Stage mentioned above.

Gandhiji had laid down that nothing should be taught to a child by force, but he should get education in everything of his interest. Play is an essential part of education, and education should appear, should be felt as a play. All education should be imparted in mother tongue, Sanskrit or Urdu as a National language. English is to be taught only as one of several other languages. No special status to be assigned to English. Religious education is indispensable.

In the Second Stage:

(a) Manual training should be continued;
(b) The boys but not the girls should be taught their parents vocation in such a way that they will by their own choice obtain their livelihood by practising the hereditary craft,
(c) The child should acquire general knowledge of world history, and geography, botany, astronomy, arithmetic, geometry, and algebra;
(d) Each child should learn how to sow and cook;
(e) Education should become self-supporting, that is, each child, all the time that he is learning, would be working upon some industry, the proceeds of which will meet the expenditure of the school, the earnings begin to flow in during the first stage itself.

Gandhiji visualized that during the third stage (16-25 years), every young person should have an education according to his or her wishes and circumstances. This statement implies that Gandhian educational system was a combination of freedom and an element of compulsion or restraint or direction.

The teacher is a very important constituent of educational system. Gandhiji was very demanding whenever the question of teacher came up. He wanted teachers to get only limited remuneration; they should not get very high salaries; they should receive only the living wage. All teachers were expected to be men of character. The economy in salaries or wages; and the simplicity and economy in infrastructural expenditure can result in making schools, colleges, etc. self-sufficient. It is a revolutionary view that education is possible even without the teacher; or it is a superstition to hold that education can be without a teacher. A man's real teacher is himself; self-education is possible today, and experiences is the biggest of schools; and, in fact, many crafts cannot be learnt in the school, they can be learnt only in workshops.

Gandhiji was of the opinion that if necessary and possible, women should use special facilities for women's education.

There should be night schools for illiterate adults. Gandhiji and others were of the firm conviction that industry in general and spinning in particular should have a pride of place in education. The education of children is primarily a duty of the parents.

Gandhiji was uneasy for a long time that present education in India was not national and as a result our people do not benefit from it, our children languish, they become incapable of any great achievement, and their knowledge does not percolate, reach to the masses. The only motivation behind education today is getting employment and making money. It is one of the fundamental principles of education that it should be planned to meet the needs of people. The present education has been a colossal failure on this count. Another basic principle of education which has been neglected in India is that education will be physical, intellectual, and religious. Therefore, he used to say confidently but with all humility that "my life is my message".

As said above, Gandhi's philosophy of education was the result of his theoretical studies, his meditation and contemplation and his experiments in the "laboratory" of life. As it has been said earlier also, his all experiments, including those relating education were comprehensive, deep, well thought out. These experiments had been conducted in South Africa and in India, they related to education of children and households, they were about curriculum, they were conducted on Tolstoy Farm and phoenix settlement or phoenix Ashram.

As a part of his experiments, Gandhiji realized the value of manual labour and spiritual training.

Gandhiji's educational experiments were partly conducted at Shantiniketan, the fact which is not widely known to the people. The Ashramas, other institutions, universities and colleges where he conducted educational experiments were: Satyagrah Ashram at Kochrab, National Gujarati School, the National Education, National Higher Education, Gujarat Vidyapith, Village Schools, Nayee Taleem, Crafts, etc.

After having presented an outline of the experiments in education by Gandhiji, let us now discuss the main lessons Gandhiji learnt, and those we can learn. Gandhiji has described and discussed his experiences and experiments at various places. They are available in a compiled book form referred to above. These are rich sources for knowing Gandhiji's philosophy of education.

It is said that the necessity is the mother of invention. Somewhat in this spirit, Gandhiji's educational experiments began out of necessity; he began to conduct them because there was no alternative for him but to start experimenting in this area.

It was January 1897 in Durban when Gandhiji landed in South Africa, and was confronted with the problem as to how to make arrangements for the education of his two sons and a nephew. For one reason or other, he did not want his children to go to either European Schools, Christian Mission Schools in Durban, the alternative of engaging the (private) English Governess.

Gandhiji's thoughts on the following aspects of education are valuable, quite exhaustive: Languages, religious education, women's education, co-education, sex education, hostels, prayers, games, exercises, and so on.

While making a case for mother tongue he had argued. "I must cling to my mother tongue as to my mother's breast in spite of its shortcomings; it alone can give me the life-giving milk. ... the mother tongue is as natural for the development of the man's mind as mother's milk is necessary for the development of infant's body."

Our language is the reflection of ourselves, and if we hold that it is too poor to express the best thought, then the sooner we are wiped out of existence the better for us.

Some quick, rough calculations have shown that every Indian youth, because he reached his knowledge through English language, lost at least six precious years of life.

If the teachers appreciate our point of view, the rural education at primary level in India should train students to be the best of first class carders, spinners, weavers, cultivators; they should know enough carpentry, they should be able to manufacture good charkhas. Such training will alone would qualify us to enter and reform village life, and this reform need not take unduly long because the fact is that "the right path is also always the shortest".

It appears that as a part of educational system particularly in rural areas in India, Gandhiji did not favour dependence on books; he did not want too many books should be published, or children should be made to read too many books. He appears to have been a believer of "oral tradition" which was the strongest in India in all time periods, particularly the ancient times.

In short, Gandhiji wanted school children to read only a few good books, to think over what they read and to put in practice what appeals to them. School education must develop in school children the ability to discriminate, which is the hallmark of real, good, and relevant education. This is the education which will benefit the students and the people of India.

The relationship between the teacher-student was of crucial importance for Gandhiji. As a part of this, he has spread a considerable amount of wisdom. He has written a lot, and has come back to this theme whenever he got the opportunity to reflect on it. He has consistently argued that it is burdening the student, if we make them learn English language. However, this did not mean that he did not want English to be taught in India at all. He did not mean that the students should stop learning English altogether. He was open that school children in India may learn English as the French men learn English. We should learn and know English as one does a foreign language. He had felt that every student in India wastes at least five years of his life in this useless endeavour:

Gandhiji was against education according to "Varna". Gandhiji has spent much of his time for explaining his views on a group of themes for which relate to each other. They are: National University, College education, State Universities, higher education, self-supporting universities, reorienting university education and new universities. His reflections on these and such themes would give us insight into Gandhiji's educational philosophy.

Gandhiji's views on Higher Education including colleges, State and National Universities have been stated above briefly.

Gandhiji's desire was to revolutionize college education and relate it to national requirements. He had visualized that colleges would be attached to the different industries which would pay for the training of the graduates they need. These colleges would function under the supervision of the State. The State would cease to run its own colleges, the private colleges including arts colleges are self-supporting, and they would remain so. Thus voluntary contributions, self-support would be the major funding patterns for colleges.

Higher education, according to Gandhiji should be left to private enterprise. The State Universities would be purely examining bodies, self-supporting through the fees charged for examinations. The universities will look after the whole field of education; they will prepare and approve courses of studies for different departments. Universities will not cost the state anything except the cost of running Central Education Department of State Government. The Universities would be self-supporting.

Gandhiji's children never went to public school, though they did get some regular schooling in an improvised school which Gandhiji started for the Satyagrahi parents in South Africa. His children never received school education, they never got graduate and post-graduate degrees, and they blamed Gandhiji for this. But the other side of these developments was that in the absence of Gandhiji's approach, the virtues of simplicity and spirit of services would have remained under-developed. They could have indulged in artificial ways of living which could have acted as a serious handicap in Gandhiji's public or social work and social services. Gandhiji did not have a sense of guilt due to the approach he adopted. He did not feel that he had not done his duty.

But the future alone will reveal as to which of these approaches is correct? In Gandhi's own words, '... the ultimate result of my experiments is in the womb of the future.' If one is allowed to hazard an assessment here, we may say that the thinking and/or behaviour and the whole life of the eldest son of Gandhiji (Hari) supports the view that it is the Gandhian thinking, Gandhian vision which will have the test of time.

Gandhiji has forewarned the people that there is a difference between disciplined home education and social education, and also of the effect produced on children through changes introduced by parents in their lives.

Truth, similarly, the votary of liberty demands sacrifices,

Gandhiji has said further that if he had been without self-respect and had satisfied us with having for my children the education that other children could not get, I should have deprived them of object-lesson in liberty and self-respect that I gave them at the cost of the literary training.

There were certain important sayings with which Gandhi used to explain his educational policy. As a part of experiments in truth and experiments in education, Gandhiji had developed certain beliefs. In South Africa, in his early years of life Gandhi had very seriously changed from the simplest to the costliest. He undertook and brought out certain changes, while introducing the changes. These changes were more internal than external.

As a part of assigning an importance to the virtues such as self-reliance, self-dependence, Gandhiji did not insist that the work should be of cleaning the closets done by the servants in the house. This proved a good training for the children and none of Gandhi's sons and other children developed aversion for scavengers work; they got a good grounding in sanitation. One of the underlying or foundational tenets of Gandhi's educational approach is that the children inherit the qualities of the parents. The educational experiments on Tolstoy Farm and phoenix settlement were necessitated by the growth of these Ashramas. There was an increase in the demand for funds which were needed in more and more quantities.

Along with character building, Gandhiji learnt from his experiments, the importance and necessity of literary training, building up of body, and vocational training. The things, the conditions, the schedules at the above-said Ashrams were so arranged that the students could get time for body-building. This is one of the very important educational lesson we get from Tolstoy and phoenix Ashrams. Education should be integrative in the sense that exercise and daily work (duty) must be interwoven with each other in such a way that they do not need separate time and resources including time. "Exercise through work" ought to be the motto of schools. The students on the Ashrams were also given vocational training (i.e. they were taught one or other useful manual vocation viz., shoe-making, carpentry, cooking).

The education on Tolstoy Farm included a wonderful rule that the students should not be asked to do what the teachers did not do.

The efforts and attention which Gandhiji gave to educate the children on Tolstoy Farm were Herculean. Although education of crafts, farming, vocational training, etc. received emphasis, the literary training also was not neglected. Gandhiji himself, along with some Ashramites taught languages to students who knew diverse languages.

Gandhiji was liked as a teacher by the students because he never attempted to disguise his ignorance from his pupils. In all respects, he showed himself to them exactly as he really was. Therefore, in spite of his ignorance of certain languages, he never lost their love and respect. Further, Gandhiji successfully taught students of different ages and learning different subjects in one and the same class room. When one reads this, one is reminded of the conditions in our schools which fit the description. The difference, however, is that while the state of Government schools is what it is because of inadequate public resources, while the conditions in Gandhian Ashrams were what they were because of self-supporting ideals of these schools.

According to Gandhiji, experience taught him that children take in much more and with less labour through their ears than through their eyes.

The physical and mental training was accompanied by spiritual training in Gandhi's Ashramas and institutions spiritual health and growth and spiritual training.

Gandhi's approach was religious, he asked students to be aware of and familiar with their scriptures, and they must be acquainted with elements of their own religion. Does it mean that Gandhiji practised secularism in his educational experiments? Basically, his approach to everything was religious or spiritual.

Gandhiji's experiments and experiences in South Africa strengthened his conviction that spiritual training was a thing by itself. The training of the spirit of the young enabled one to work towards the knowledge of God and self-realization, and all that training without culture of the spirit was of no use, and it may even harm education.

6

General Educational Philosophy of Mahatma Gandhi and Vinoba Bhave

The Chapter Six as a core chapter of this book on Educational Philosophy of Gandhiji and Vinobaji contains the discussion on many themes and subthemes which would help to understand the educational philosophy of Gandhiji and Vinobaji.

It discusses the meaning, aims, goals, objectives of education, the basic principles and characteristics of education, sources of philosophy, the basic principles, elements, tenets. The presentation is rather loose, and the nature of the subject has required a greater space. With these introductory remarks, we begin the discussion with defining the keywords which occur during the discourse.

Philosophy

Philosophy, as per the Concise Oxford Dictionary, is the use of reason and argument in seeking truth and knowledge of reality, particularly the nature and causes of things. It comprises principles governing existence, the material universe, the perception of physical phenomenon and human behaviour. It is a personal rule of life. Philosopher is a person engaged or learned in philosophy. When this becomes applicable with a focus to a given area, that area is designated as, say "philosophy of psychology"; or "philosophy of language", or economic philosophy.

The term philosophy has two parts—philos (love) and sophi (wisdom). After joining them we get philosophy which means love of wisdom. Philosophy also means persistent attempts to give insight into the nature of the world by means of reflection. Philosophy primarily aims at knowledge; it is the search for understanding of values and reality. It is an intellectual quest for truth. Philosophy is the oldest of discipline, the mother discipline; it is the root of all knowledge.

Lucas has opined that philosophy is a personal attitude towards life and universe. It is about doubt, wonder, and curiosity. It is reflective or speculative thinking. It grows out of our awareness of the problem of existence. Philosophy is an attempt to gain a view of the whole life.

Educational Philosophy (EP)

When philosophy is engaged in reflecting on key issues and concepts in education, it is called philosophy of education (POE). POE may mean academic field of applied philosophy and/or it may mean any one of philosophies that promote a specific type or vision of education and/or which examine the definition, goals and meaning of education. POE is philosophical study of education, and its central subject matter is education. POE may be about the process of education. It can also be understood as a normative educational theory that unifies pedagogies, curriculum, learning theory. These theories are also called educational philosophies.

Education

The next word to be defined is education. The dictionary meaning of education is a systematic instruction and development of character and mental powers. This meaning of education is unsatisfactory; it is marred by tautology.

But it is not easy to get over this problem. An apparently simple term education has proved to be quite complex and difficult. There is no consensus, let apart unanimity, among educationists in respect of defining education. Gandhiji has said in this regard, that the real difficulty is that people have no ideas of what education truly is. We assess the value of education in the same manner as we assess the land or shares. We hardly give any thought to the improvement of the character of the educated. As long as such ideas persist, there is no hope of ever knowing in true value of education.

This is well reflected in different people defining education differently. Education has been defined as literacy, as training, as service, as liberation, as assimilation, as contemplation, as self-discipline, etc.

According to Dayle, J.F. (January 1973), the core of Gandhi philosophy is (1) The truth, (2) Morality, (3) Violence, (4) Non-violence, (5) Detachment, (6) Society, and (7) Direct Action.

According to Vinoba, the goal of education is to avoid spending on stilted buildings, to avoid increasing only the literacy rate, to ensure that indigenous craft is not neglected, and to make religious education with high priority.

Etymologically, the word education is derived from Latin word. In fact, there are two words in the word, education. They are "e" and "due" and they mean "out of" or "to lead", respectively. The word education means "to bring out from inside". Some scholars trace the root of education—"educare" and "educaer"; the former meaning development, and latter meaning enhancement or improvement and progress. According to this root, education means the art of developing and enhancing, cultivating the various physical, mental and moral powers of the learner. Education, therefore, is a life-long process rather than a product.

In our view, the best definition, the best meaning of education has been given by Vinoba and Sane Guruji in their respective poems reproduced below:

POEM 1 (MARATHI)

Shikshak Ani Mulay
Doghehi Yekmekancha
AAcharana pasoon Shikat Asatat
Doghehi Vydyarthich AAhet
Je Dilejat nahi te shikshan
Je ghetale jate
Jyacha hisheb Thevala Jawaoo Shakato
Kinwa Jyachi Kanni nonda
Thevali Jawoo Shakte
Te Shikshan Navech
Jivanach Shikshan Aahe
Caloricha Khara hisheb
Kagdavarch Nawhe
Shariravar disoon Aashashuch
Je experienced, Je Khallye, pachele
Raktatmurale, tech shikshat — Vinoba

POEM 2 (MARATHI-TRANSLATION)

To plough land
With one hand
Is better than hundred lectures
Or to spin khadi with one hand
Is far better than "Mantra Japa"
To colour one
(piece) of cloth is better
Than erudition —Sane Guruji

The liberal approach and translation from Marathi to English would enable the reader to fathom the nature and meaning of education.

There are two sides to education: the teacher and children. Both of them educate themselves by observing the behaviour of each other. Both of them are students only. The thing which cannot be given is true education. The thing which can be taken is not education. The thing whose account can be kept is not education. Life itself is education. The true count of calories is not kept on paper, it is kept on body. Whatever we experience, whatever we eat and digest, whatever gets absorbed and assimilated in the blood is only education.—Vinoba

An important point Gandhi and Vinoba have consistently and repeatedly stressed is the role, place, and knowledge of Alphabet. There is a clear difference of the position of the Government on the one hand, and Gandhi and Vinoba on the other. The Government has always thought that its education policy has been successful if the literacy rate has increased. G-V have argued that mere knowledge of letters is not enough, the literacy rate is the least important indicator of educational progress. Vinoba used to point out that saints like Kabir gave so much wisdom because they were illiterate. Knowledge of alphabet may be useful if it is service-oriented (seva parayan). Knowledge of mere alphabet does not increase the ethical/moral level by even an inch.

Gandhi's philosophy of basic education was also a factor in his design for a New India. Thus Basic Education (BE) meant New Education. Gandhi perceived education as a method of social reconstruction. By involving the child as a participant in an interacting educational and productive group, BE could counteract the ingrained Indian attitude that relegated physical labour to lower castes and current anti-social individualism.

BE would, Gandhi believed, inculcate the spirit of co-operative unity and group responsibility. In his perception, the school was a miniature society; he thought BE as providing a common educational foundation that would reduce the gap between urban and rural India.

Gandhi was direct in rejecting Western, modern civilization and he outrightly rejected the doctrines "Might is Right" and "Survival of the fittest". According to him Western Education was a "rotten" and "false" education. He believed that English education had enslaved India.

Gandhi's social philosophy and ideas on BE favoured the child belong to the lowest structure of society. Tolstoy Farm model was to teach pupils to conquer hate by love, untruth by truth, and violence by self-sacrifice.

Gandhi rejects all modernist distinctions such as "is" and "ought" or science and faith, etc. which has been taken to mean that he was returning to pre-modern modes of thought. He reaffirms his own Hindu traditions that the goal of human life should be Truth and virtue rather than wealth and power. He appears to be in agreement with pre-modernism that the body and senses are a hindrance to the spiritual life. He never speaks of the world as illusory. He frequently affirmed a strict dualism between soul and body and between our spiritual nature and animal nature. The body is given to us because of our karma; we are enslaved in the body because of our sinful deeds. The body, a filthy mass of bones, flash, and blood; when it is under the control of God, it is a jewel, but when it passes to the control of devil, it is a pit of filth. When MK Gandhi talks of a person's spiritual development, it is not a passive or static affair. Gandhi emphasized very often the unity of heart, mind, body, and spirit.

Gandhi believed in the integrity of the individual. The individual is the supreme consideration. He feared the power of the State because it does the greatest harm to mankind by destroying individuality, which was at the root of all progress.

The doctrine of karma is modernist in assuming the concept of individual moral responsibility. Gandhi's experiments for Truth are distinctively modernist with their firm assumption that the individual is the final arbiter of action; Gandhi also rejects a pre-modern cyclical view of history in favour of modernist view of linear moral progression. A very modernist Gandhi has stated that the force of spirit is ever progressive and endless. This viewpoint undermines pre-modern view that one should train in the profession of one's father.

Gandhi's conception of religion also can be called modernist. He believed that all religions are equal, their essence is the same. According to Gandhiji, religion is purely a personal matter, and there are as many religions as there are individuals. He also appears to be committed to the modernist reduction of religion to ethics.

Instead of using the term anarchist, Gandhi could be called communitarian, and doing so would mean that Gandhi was post-modern.

Gandhi's appeal to reason and scientific method ties him to Modern World View. He was firmly committed to the method of rational inquiry and experimental testing. He said that we must reject truth claims, even those of scriptures, that are repugnant to reason or moral sense. Gandhi was a modernist and Western world-view holder.

Gandhi has qualified his individualism with other constitution and he going in the post-modern construction of the self. Gandhi's aesthetic is in significant agreement with the view that his aesthetics of virtue is part and parcel of the best ethics for constructive post-modernism. Gandhi belongs with the constructive post-modernists. Similarly, the proposition Truth is God is an attempt to overcome the modernist critique of religion. Gandhi's post-modern religion is all-encompassing.

Gandhi's religion could be integrated nicely with his post-modern communitarianism. Gandhi's reasons for rejecting other Indian Nationalists' programmes can best be interpreted as constructive post-modernism. Gandhi's fusion of means and ends, the inner and outer religion and politics is neither pre-modern nor not modern, but post-modern.

Vinoba Bhave's thoughts on education are well-grounded and practical in nature, and it has ennobling effect. Both these traits are conspicuous by their absence in the present day mainstream education.

Gandhi-Vinoba have been the greatest philosophers of education, the greatest teachers of mankind in the line of Mahavira, Buddha, Shankaracharya, Vivekananda, etc. Their Basic Scheme of Education (BSE) or Nai Talim remains the most valuable legacy that they have left for the mankind.

A few definitions of Education are: [More definitions/quotes on education may be obtained from Appendix. In the text, only a limited number of quotes have been given for ready reference.]

(1) Education is the manifestation of divine perfection already existing in man.—Vivekanand
(2) Education is something which makes one self-reliant and selfless. Ancient Indian concept of education highlights higher knowledge, freedom from ignorance, salvation, and self-realization.—Rig Veda
(3) Education is an instrument for character formation and righteous living.—Swami Dayananda
(4) Education enables man to find out the ultimate truth.—Rabindranath Tagore
(5) The ultimate aim of education is self-realization, true education draws out and stimulates the spiritual aspect.
(6) T.S. Eliot did not find teaching altogether palatable, and he found that for him teaching was not a preferred activity. As he has said, "I have never worked in a coal mine, or a uranium mine, but I know from my experience that working in bank was a best cure compared to teaching in a school."
(7) Education is an all-round drawing out the best in child and in man. Education is meant for all round human development. The optimum enrichment and development of personality should be achieved through education.—Gandhi
(8) Education is a gift for life. It is certainly a means for all-round development of man. The pathway to human development or progress goes through education. Education is the whole basis of achieving the purpose in life. It is the means for developing personality of individual, it makes life purposeful. It makes us self-sufficient. It makes man efficient, and skillful.
(9) Education is a technique of transmitting civilization.
(10) According to Upnishads, education means salvation.
(11) Education means "darshan".

The Aims of Education

(1) It should develop higher values in life, (2) It should develop a sense of Common National ethos and qualities of citizenship,

(3) Develop positive attitudes, (4) Social responsibilities, (5) Vocational efficiencies, (6) Not to pour information into the heads of people.

Thus, the purpose of education is character building, change in attitudes, and values, optimum enrichment, personality development, social, political, economic development or change, intellectual development. Education is regarded to be instrumental for the survival of traditions, for continuation of the culture. Education means freedom or liberation. It is said to enable us to preserve our "dharma" or "Paramdharma" or "Moksha". The education enables us to assimilate what we get. It imparts religious and moral instruction. The true education helps people to practise the tenets like "know thyself".

As the man grows, he develops his physical, mental, emotional growth. Through education, man tends to become mature in all respects, he develop sense of responsibility. Education is vitally necessary to achieve the growth and development of both the individual and societies.

Education has been one of the most crucial foundation stones of any civilization and culture. If the present, modern civilization and culture and social orders are to survive, education is one of the means. Education not only moulds the new generation, but also reflects society's fundamental assumptions about itself.

The education that obstructs freedom must be shunned because it is satanic and sinful. The true education helps to assimilate what we get; it imparts religious and moral instruction, and it helps to overcome fear from even the God. The true or real education helps people to practise "know thyself", it gives you spiritual experience; the soul, "Aatmasakshatkar", or "self-realization", and "Mukti".

Gandhi-Vinoba have been criticized that their thoughts, ideas, principles, values, etc. are no longer relevant for our times. They have been pioneers in leading struggles against racism, colonialism, casteism. They have been the promoters of true democratic values, swaraj, third power, etc. As long as there is a strife, hostility, ethnic strifes, religious unrest and so on, G-V will remain relevant.

Gandhi-Vinoba believed that to educate the man wholly, education needs to be craft-centered, which will lead to the highest development of mind, intellect and soul. The craft-chosen for instruction should be manual and productive and area of the school. The framework for this education should be co-operative activity, etc. For MKG, craft-centeredness is significant spiritually so, it is said that the notion of education through craft rose from the contemplation on Truth and Love. Craft-centered education helps to develop an all-round personality in which action, knowledge, and feelings are evenly balanced. Such an education will help in achieving objectives such as "bread and butter", and "Moral aim".

Craft-centered method of education is consistent with the primacy of non-violence. It is hoped that such an education will bring a "New Age" from which elites and communal hatred will be eliminated. This education again balances the space for individual and collective co-operativeness.

Gandhi-Vinoba had realized that modern education had completely failed. This modern education should be thoroughly revolutionized. Towards this goal, to begin with he introduced education in handicrafts in the "Ashram-Shallas".

The rationale Gandhiji proposed for the introduction of production process was that schools must be self-supporting for two reasons: First, the poor society could not provide education to all children unless schools could generate the physical and financial resources to run them. Second, the financial self-sufficiency alone could protect schools from dependence on the State.

The values of self-sufficiency, and autonomy were close to Gandhi and Vinoba's heart. Financial self-sufficiency was linked to truth, and autonomy to non-violence.

Responding to the charge that he was against higher education, Gandhiji pointed out that the charge was false because he was in favour of giving any higher of the highest education that existed in the world. Wherever there is utility of education to the state, the state should bear the educational expenses. He was against providing funds from the state account. Further, he has explained that it is his firm belief that the education of literature which is being given in Indian higher school is too costly. This system results in the wastage of energy. The too much literary education has resulted in creating more and more unemployment in the educated groups. The most important, dangerous, and worrisome matter is that increasing number of college-going young people have tended to lose the physical and mental health.

Similarly, the use of foreign language in education at higher levels has harmed the educational sector in India. It has resulted in intellectual and moral degradation. On the basis of his experience, he has argued that whatever knowledge he obtained till the age of 12 years was obtained through mother tongue as medium of instruction. Educational philosophy assumes that (1) Knowledge resides within the individual himself and perfection is already inherent in man. (2) The child does his own growing. The child teaches himself. Gandhi believed that our duty is to afford opportunities, and to remove obstacles. Gandhi, like Vivekananda believed in the importance of self-education. Nothing should be forced upon children. They should be left to themselves to carry out their own path. And undue domination exercised on them will mar their development. (3) Gandhi's thinking of education is founded on philosophical beliefs, the soul is immortal, man is subject to rebirth; matter is subordinate to mind.

Gandhi-Vinoba presents a radical critique and alternative to the dominant characteristics of modern, Western civilization and the contemporary world. Is Gandhiji's philosophical orientation more pre-modern, modern or post-modern? Both have been critique of modern thinking. They do not call for a simple, religious, mythic narrative or philosophical return to some past. We cannot classify Gandhi's philosophy as pre-modern or modern or post-modern. His philosophy is syncretic, eclectic, the philosophy of the autonomous individual. Their philosophy was not inspired by constitution; it was inspired by religious, spiritual thought.

In Nai Talim, Gandhi-Vinoba evolved a scheme of education which would be in harmony with the culture and civilization of the Indian people. The craft work can help the child to acquire sensor and metor co-ordination and to appreciate the value of honest labour. The craft as the centre of education is desirable psychological because it relieved the child from tyranny of a purely academic and theoretical instruction against which its active nature is always making a protest. This feature of Nai Talim (to make practical and productive work) in which all children of the nation will participate, will lead to breakdown of the existing barriers of prejudice between manual and intellectual worker's harmful alike for both the NT, if carried out intelligently and efficiently, the Nai Talim scheme will increase the productive capacity.

The foundational value system in which they had full faith

made G-V trenchant, vehement critics of the modern Western education in particular, and industrial civilization in general.

Gandhi-Vinoba philosophy is a blend of idealism and core practice. The sources of inspiration of their philosophy were primarily ancient Indian scriptured texts. Their unflinching faith in Truth, ahimsa and other twelve *"vratas"* or vows constitute the firm foundation of his general and educational philosophy.

The next feature of their philosophy refers to the principle of learning and earning through daily manual work.

Their ideas, experiments, and various aspects of education are bound with "constructive works programme" needed badly for Swaraj as well as peoples' self-reliance. Similarly, the principle of learning and earning through daily manual work has been an essential part of their philosophy.

According to G-V philosophy, the goal(s) of education were a mix of narrow functional, and at the same time highly elevated goals. It was expected to contribute to earnings of independence, to promote justice, equality, revival of villages, reinstatement of Indian culture, eliminate caste system, unify knowledge and action. The goal of Gandhian revolution was creation of a new social order. This required new education, Nai Talim was such a new education. Wardha scheme as such does not include the total G-V philosophy because that scheme is concerned with the education of children between the ages of 7 to 14 only.

Gandhi-Vinoba's stand for a harmonious development of all the four aspects of human personality (body, mind, heart, spirit) also needs to be noted. Their education ideal must mean total development of total system. Education with vocational training is one of the most important aspect of their philosophy of education. The creed of Ahimsa and culture of peace are the fundamental aspects of their philosophy.

There can be two approaches to values, schemes, projects, etc. One is to regard it as a principle, and the other is to treat it as perfunctory. They chose to adopt the first approach which emphasized the principle aspect of the value. Charka was a tool, but it also was a philosophy. Satyagraha, non-violence was a technique, but it was also a principle, while other Indian political leaders accepted, adopted non-violence as merely a technique, Gandhiji always emphasized its principle aspect.

"The educational system should be self-reliant," they argued, in curriculum craft(s) would be an indispensable part. In their manual labour and philosophical values of self-reliance were accorded great importance.

Their belief in Advaitic philosophy led them to destroy all false boundaries. For example, segregation and untouchability, rural-urban divide, superiority of intellectual labour over the manual labour, primary education for the villages, secondary education in the cities, and higher education in universities, all such divides were rejected by them. They argued that everyone should have equal access to any type of education he or she desired.

Gandhi-Vinoba's views on language issue clearly reflect that they took a stand on issues based on certain values, philosophical considerations. Among other things, this detailed examination of multiple considerations regarding the language policy clearly reflects this. An important aspect of their philosophy of education is their view of the importance of the language used as the medium of instruction in schools and colleges.

Gandhi-Vinoba's insistence on education through mother tongue or the issue of appropriate, correct, desirable medium of instruction was founded on the philosophy and also the psychology of the learners. They wanted the entire educational system in India to be overhauled and replaced by the alternative system which would be a welfare-enhancing; it would eliminate the duality, help the masses, reduce and subsequently eliminate all types of economic, social, geographical regional inequalities, and exploitation.

Gandhi-Vinoba's insistence, supported by many Indian and foreign scholars, on the use of vernaculars had its origin in various economic, social, psychological, practical values, considerations, factors.

The sources of their philosophy were primarily the self. At the same time, they had read much, much more than the so called "intellectuals". Vinoba was a voracious reader and on his own authority, we know that he had read thousands of books by his matriculation. The following external sources played an important role in shaping the (educational) their philosophy.

Indian philosophy, Mahabharat, Bhagvad Gita, Ramayan, Bhagavat, Ved-Vedanta, the literature of Saints, dharma shastras. They believe in the philosophy of "Aano bhadraha kratuo yentu sarvataha." One can say that they practised "Window Strategy".

They favoured neither the fully opened doors of houses, nor completely closed-doors policy. They wanted houses with walls and windows for the purpose of circulation. They had a very clear, unambiguous stand on the modern West vis-à-vis "Bhartiya Sanskriti and culture". They were not enamoured by the "growth" of the West. They said that ultimately India alone guides the destiny of the world.

"The educational system should be self-reliant," Gandhi argued, the preparation of the curriculum in which craft(s) would be an indispensable, essential part. Gandhism was due to the importance given to philosophical values of self-reliance, importance of manual labour.

If the objectives just mentioned are to be achieved, we would have to move from simple, conventional education to "life-education", and for this to happen, we will have to impart spiritual on a greater and greater scale today, the condition of whole humanity is as described by Ishavasyopnished as follows:

Thus, what is required to be done is to do away the cover of materialism from the truth through people's education (Lokshikshan), and we have to give importance to spiritual education. We have to create capacity to understand the real economic, social, and political values of the common people. Through education, we must bring about the values-change.

Gandhi's philosophy of education is a theistic, spiritual philosophy. As a part of the work of searching for New Educational Paradigm, the contribution of Gandhi-Vinoba stands alone. In their educational philosophy there is harmony between speech and action. This is well-illustrated by "sugar story" or "sugar syndrome".

It is difficult to categorize Gandhi-Vinoba in terms of schools and philosophy. They are neither modern, pre-modern nor post-modern. For them, most of the post and 20th century philosophy is a kind of oppressive, unjustified, reductionist that presents a narrow, impoverished view of existence. He has also recognized the importance of non-rational in life.

Gandhi has been the best-known proponent of Ahimsa and Truth both in personal life and in political sphere. What were the ideological, philosophical foundations of non-violence and Truth which he propounded? Although one cannot be definitive, it is possible to say that there is some coherent philosophy in the mind of Gandhi when he preached Non-violence and Truth. Gandhi gave exalted positions to Truth and Non-violence (NV) although they were known earlier also. For him, the truth had the highest value as an end, and that NV is valuable because it serves as best means of achieving truth. Truth simply refers to reality. He extended the concept of Truth to moral beliefs. For Gandhi, Truth is the highest good, it is the natural goal of our existence. His famous equation in this context has been Truth is God and God is Truth.

The education is too important to be left to the market forces. Naturally, we will have to develop ideas, virtues, values which will make an honest, genuine improvement in education. Gandhi-Vinoba philosophy of education was religious; it was spiritual and not secular. The most of the people in at least India unhesitatingly, openly believed that God or creator was the Almighty powerful phenomenon. Thus, theirs was a theistic philosophy. They positively believed that God exists.

The role and importance of education cannot be gainsaid. The teacher is not only the nuclei of the education system, but is also the backbone of the system and the success and failure of this system depends to a large extent on the community of teachers. A teacher, if works with sincerity, honesty, and sense of duty, raises students to their total development.

The basic tenets of educational reforms have been succinctly stated by Gandhi and Tagore. Gandhi has said, "The growth is the movement of a whole to a fuller wholeness. The living things possess this wholeness from the beginning. A child has its own perfection as a child ... childhood is not merely a waiting room for manhood. Children have a life of their own, with its own values and its own rewards and those grow most successfully into ripe man and woman who savour their childish life to the full while they have it. They grow by being themselves. (M. Sykes, pp. 8-9)

Some of the most original enterprises of our time have been carried on by Tagore, Gandhi, Vinoba, etc. Some contemporary educational thinkers have put forth ideas on these lines, as a constructive alternative to the institutional rigidity of our prevailing pattern of "higher education", "De-schooling", "Free Universities", "Open Universities". All these are manifestations of a search for something better. (M. Sykes pp. 12-13).

In the riddle of the sphinx, the answer is Man. The sphinx is saying that he can save mankind. The most important answer the man gives to the most difficult question with which he is confronted is man himself. (M. Sykes, pp. 12-13)

- According to Rousseu and Vinoba, there are three parts of educations *Nisarga*-education; *Vyakti*-education; and *Vyavaharic*-education.
- In education, we should learn Yoga, Udyoga, and Sahayoga.

Gandhi-Vinoba added a number of completely new ideas such as collective sarva-dharma prayers, khadi, collective sadhana, and so forth. The reader's attention may be drawn to the idea of three r's and three h's as given below:

- Hand—psychometer domain
- Heart—spiritual
- Head—Cognitive domain I skills

In Indian tradition, philosophy is "darshana" to see or seeing. It means spiritual perception. "Darshana" is a spiritual perception, "Darshana" means true knowledge or reliable knowledge. Manu has called philosophy a "samyak Darshana", knowledge leading to salvation, without which man cannot free himself from earthly bondage. According to Radhakrishnan, "Darshana" is a logical exposition of the nature of reality (Ganiher, p. 127). The word "darshan" itself symbolizes visual knowledge. Scriptures speak of "spiritual vision". For perception of abstract things intellectual eyes are used. Scriptures speak of "spiritual vision" or "divine eye" which is capable of seeing the most obscure thing.

Adhyatmic or Spiritual Education

According to Gandhi-Vinoba, the aim of education is to create a spiritual social order. Vinoba has also suggested that it is the responsibility of teachers to bring about revolution in the field of education. What is spirituality? What is meant by Adhyatm Vichar?

There are five "Nishtas" of Spirituality:

(1) To have faith in moral, ethical values.
(2) The unity and purity of all living beings.
(3) Life exists after death.
(4) The fruit of karma (Karma vipak) exists.
(5) There is arrangement, organization, stability in the Universe.

Salvation is the goal of life. Mukti means becoming egoless. Moksha, Moha, Sakshatkar, "Bhagwat darshan" are aspects of spirituality. It should be always remembered that spirituality is different from any "dharma pantha". The goal of dharma is to take man towards spirituality.

Gandhi-Vinoba's philosophy of education is greatly inspired by the *Vratas*, Purusharthas, Varnas, spirituality, and Ashramas.

Within the Adhyatmic way of life, the practice or observance of *vratas* has been of great importance and relevance for constructing philosophy of life and philosophy of education. Vrat-vichar, vrat chintan, vrat sadhana have served as philosophical foundation of activities in various fields. Gandhi-Vinoba's philosophy of education has been founded on these Indian traditions, and values.

Ekadasha vrataha:

> *Ahimsa, Satya, Asteya, Brahmacharya, Asangraha* ||
> *Shareer shrama, Aswad* | *Sarvatra Bhaya varjanam* ||
> *Sarva-Dharmi samamtava, Swadeshi Sparsha bhavana* ||
> *Vinamra Vrat Nishtase, Ye Ekadash Savya He* ||

Ekadasha vratas had also been called "jiven shuddhi Sadhana" or "Satyagraha Nishta". In ancient times, the reference used to be to only five *vratas* (Panch-Sheel), and they were meant to be practised by individuals. It is to Gandhi's credit that he reinforced the power of system of *Vratas* by adding more *vratas* making them eleven. The other change he introduced was to teach the people that this set of *vratas* is as relevant for individual sadhana as "social sadhana". The list of those *Vratas* along with their meaning is briefly given below:

(1) "Asteya" means much more than non-stealing or the absence of theft in the common sense terms. That one should not use various things including the necessities of life without participating in the process of their production, that one should not pay others less than the right wages, that one should not expect to receive services from others at cheap rates, at least one should not take or receive something from others without giving something in return are all included in "asteya". Any act of consumption or enjoyment without some sacrifice amounts to stealing. "Asteya" is very much necessary to create an equitable, non-exploitative and just social order.

(2) "Brahmacharya" or continence in its ultimate sense denotes that life-style which helps the individual to attain "Brahman" (God). It encompasses many things that one should not covet women other than one's own wife, nay, one should regard other women as one's mothers or sisters, that the married person should desire his wife only for procreation, that one should lead a life of self-restraint in all spheres, and that one should endeavour to attain a full control over all the senses and desires. The relevance of this "vrata" for non-violent social order is too obvious to need an elaboration.

(3) "Aparigraha" or non-possession, or "asangraha" or non-accumulation stresses the value of minimization of wants, simplicity of life, and voluntary poverty. Like birds and animals, man also need not and ought not to accumulate material things including the necessities of life. This "vrata" solves man's Hamletian dilemma or confusion about "to have or not to have". It is direct answer to the problem of disparities, exploitation, and violence in the modern acquisitive, accumulating, achieving, possessive, and materialistic societies.

(4) "Sharirashram" or "bread labour" means that absolutely everyone must undertake manual or physical work of some kind or other at least a few hours every day. Everyone has an entitlement to his daily bread only by the "sweat of his brow". The basis of this is that the bodily labour is the only natural means of the daily upkeep of the body. The separation between the intellectual (mental) work and the manual work, and the culture of superiority of the former over the latter are artificial and harmful developments. Both of these types of work can be more effective, productive, and enjoyable only if there is a balanced mix of them every day. Gandhi regarded bread labour as an effective means of self-restraint and egalitarianism.

(5) "Aswad" or the control of the palate is thought necessary for the successful observance of many other *"vratas"*, particularly "brahmacharya", and for the success in "sadhana", i.e., efforts towards self-realization or self-liberation. In India, mind, spiritual progress, and the emancipation or liberation of the self or soul is stressed.

Gandhi added the next six *"vratas"* after taking into account the demands of modern times and the contemporary conditions in India. He had made the recitation of eleven *"vratas"* compulsory during the daily morning and evening prayers in his "ashrams" or abodes of social workers. In fact, he regarded the observance of these "*vratas*" as necessary not only for the "ashramites" but also for everybody in the ordinary business of life; he saw in them the only means for the liberation of both the individual self and the social self. The last (Twelth) "vrata" was added by Vinoba.

The observance of these twelve "*vratas*" can lay the foundation of a non-violent social order because they can eliminate the inner or psychic sources of agitation, excitement, emotion, provocation, irritation, and violence, or they can effectively control the urge or craving for money, wealth, power, fame, and carnal desires. The basic prerequisite for a non-violent society is the peace within the individuals; the peace without is possible only when the peace within reigns. Man cannot be an instrument of peace unless he is at peace with himself. The "dwadash *vratas*" help man to achieve this peace within himself and thereby help in creating a peaceful social system.

For example, the free play of greed makes people compulsive competitors which creates exploitative and conflicting relationship between them. Certain "*vratas*" control the greed in man; they equip him to unhinge himself from the pursuit of material acquisitions, and to concentrate on service, sacrifice, altruism, and other spiritual values or motivations. They also instill in him the respect for the "will to live" in other beings. All this tends to eliminate man's violence against all living beings and the Nature.

(6) Ahimsa or non-violence means non-killing or non-injury at the physical as well as mental levels. It connotes that we should not only not cause pain, sorrow, injury, and death to other beings but also that we should love them. To abjure aggressive as well as self-protective violence and to be compassionate towards others are parts of "ahimsa". Gandhi used to say that "ahimsa" means universal love, and that love is the fundamental law of our being. He practised and taught others to practise the following progressive law of non-violence given by Christ: "Forgive others. Love each other as I love thee. Love thy neighbour as thyself. Love thy enemy."

(7) Satya: Gandhi gave the utmost importance to "satya" or truth as the basis of life at all levels. He had sub-titled his autobiography as the "Experiments with Truth", and he remained a life-long friends.

(8) "Abhaya" or fearlessness is also an essential quality for the establishment and success of a non-violent social order. The indomitable human spirit and the freedom from fear of anything including death are basic to an ethical lifestyle. In the Gandhian social order, a truly fearless human being would not lift an arm to strike anyone for self-protection or for protecting others. He would achieve these things through soul force.

(9) "Sarvadharma samanatva" or "Sarvadharma sambhava" means equal acceptance, affection and love, (and not merely equal respect and tolerance as under secularism), for all religions, faiths, beliefs, creeds, sects, and "panthas". It teaches us that each religion is incomplete in some sense and yet each one is true; that behind some conceptual and external differences, there is a basic unity among all the religions in the world; and that they lead us to the same goal. We must learn to see the merits and demerits, and accept the merits and correct the demerits of all religions including our own religion. This would transform the blind love into an enlightened and "satvik" (pure, virtuous) love for one's own religion, and would nurture the universal or cosmic or catholic vision of man. It must be noted that the Gandhian vision of "Sarvadharma sambhava" is entirely different from the ideology of secularism. While the former will certainly eliminate communal violence, the latter is altogether incapable of achieving such a result.

(10) "Sparshabhavana" means touchability or the absence of untouchability. At a certain juncture in history, the Hindu social order came to be stricken with the curse of untouchability; it rendered even the touch of the body and shadow of a person from the "lower" castes a matter of defilement and taboo for the person belonging to the "upper" castes. The "lower-caste" people came to be forbidden from visiting and praying inside the Hindu temples. The practitioner of "Sparshabhavana" would renounce the feelings of untouchability and superiority-inferiority in respect of different social groups and professions.

He would regard everyone as his equal and brother.

Though invented in the context of the Hindu society and the typical communal problems in India, "Sarvadharma sambhava" and "Sparshabhavana" have far wider relevance and applications. They constitute a solution to similar problems in other societies because basically they teach equality between man and man. They lay the foundation of a truly democratic, liberal, egalitarian, and peaceful social order. Through these *"vratas"*, Gandhi taught the whole world that the injustice and violence against the labour, the poor, the women, the Negroes, the scheduled castes and tribes, and other religious communities can be eliminated only by becoming compassionate towards them, and not by arousing the passions of castes, classes, sexes, races, and religions.

(11) "Swadeshi" literally would mean love or preference for things of one's own country. In its wider sense, it denotes many goals such as self-sufficiency and self-reliance at the local level, day-to-day living in the ordinary business of life; it teaches that things, traditions, from near ought to be dear to us.

(12) "Aninda" or non-criticism, strictly speaking, is included in "ahimsa", but for Vinoba it is necessary to add it as an explicit or separate "vrata" in order to overcome a weakness in human nature. "Aninda" means not seeing faults or defects or vices of others and not blaming or criticizing others for their faults. It also means recognizing, and concentrating on the merits or virtues of others, and inducing others to become by magnifying their virtues. The basis of this "vrata" is that since I am also full of defects, I have no moral right to criticize others for their defects, and that defects are of the body of the soul, and, therefore, they are not of the individual. Aninda also means concentrate one's own virtues rather than defects. The observance of this "vrata" would result in round "Guna Vikas", i.e., the flourishing of virtues in all human beings, and this would peace and happiness in the society.

After discussing the contents of eleven or twelve *vratas*, we should discuss the role of three types of institutions whose functioning had contributed to the development of the role of these institutions in the Indian education. They are: Ashram (2 types) and Varna-Purusharth (4).

Together, they were widely known as "Varna Shram Dharma" or "varnashram system" or "varnashram vyavastha". The three components of this system or arrangements were as follows:

Ashram 1: Places, institutions where formal and informal education was imparted.

Ashram 2: The arrangements or division of time span of life of individuals such that each part had its own special functions, tasks or karmas, or "Dharma", viz., Brahmacharyashram, Grihisthashram, Vanprasthashram, and Sanyasashram.

- Varna. The division of the society in four parts or components; the persons belonging to a given component or part had to perform certain functions in which they had become experts or specialized. There were four varnas, namely Brahmin, Kshatriya, Vaisha, and Shudra.
- The varnashram dharma is the unique system of organization of the life of individual and society, respectively. In no other country such an institution exist or existed in any period of history, that in ancient India, the Ashramas of different Rishis, Yogis, Munis dotted the forests and those Ashramas were engaged in diverse activities. It is a happy matter that the tradition of Ashrams has remained alive even today. They have kept this system alive.

Elements of philosophy of education of Gandhiji and Vinobaji (collected):

1) *Sharirik shiksha* (physical education): To cook, cleanliness—grinding, to fetch water; exercise, science of health.
2) Industrial (*kalpa*): Spinning, agriculture, stitching, carpentry.
3) *Bhashik* (Language and grammar): Sanskrit, one's own language, language of others.
4) Social or *samajik*: Politics, sociology, economics, history.
5) *Kalatmak*: Music, drawing etc.
6) *Vyavaharik (Jyotish)*: Geographic, material sciences.
7) Another grand phenomenon in our education is the last meeting of students with Guru. He tells students as follows:

   For 12 years, you got some *vidya* from me. But do not regard my teachings as standard. Let truth be the only standard. You examine my words and my actions against Truth. Truth is the ultimate.
8) Education should promote Ahimsa.
9) Education should be independent of the state and the rich.
10) The police should not be allowed to enter educational institutions at any time.
11) The whole country is like university campus, there should be no police on the campus, therefore, the police should not enter/exist in the country.

In India, education was everywhere in ancient times (sarvatra).

12) *Dnan* (vidya) to be obtained through hearing (shravan) as far as possible; rather than speaking. Shruti, Smriti, kruti is Indian shikshan Shastra.
13) The goal of pupils should be to become "vratsnatak" and not merely "vidyasnatak"
14) *Vidya* leads to humility. Pupils should be humble, and they should make people also humble.
15) *Vidya* must result in making pupils courageous also.
16) An important aspect of education is study in early morning, and self-study (swadhyaya) is a very essential aspect of education.
17) It is indeed a grand thought that we need both *Vidya* and Avidya.
18) Vedas are the soul of education in Indian tradition.
19) The teachers can change the thinking, hearts, mind, and life of the people.
20) The school is not a place for imparting education; it is a place where development of the individual (vyakti vikas) takes place.
21) Education must be based on experience.
22) Education should be free, compulsory, liberated, autonomous, beyond the state.
23) The revival of 'Bhartiya shikshan shastra' is today's imperative; it is to be underlined that it is constituted by the enlightenment from Shri Krishna, Gandhi, Vinoba and others. The "Bhartiya Shikshan Shastra" and "Bhartiya Dharmashastra" are a complete guide to the individual and society.
24) We must honestly exert to actualize the ideas "Vishwa Bharti" (by Rabindranath Tagore) and "Aanterbharti" (by Sane Guruji).
25) Education must integrate activities (karma) and knowledge (dnana).
26) Unitarian and equalitarian approaches. If India and the world (mankind) wish to develop, there should be oneness, unity, union of karma and Dnana is essential.
27) The Gandhi-Vinoba "Shikshan Vichar" is very much radical, nay revolutionary; it is in keeping with Bhartiya Sanskriti; culture, tradition.

28) Vinoba has coined a number of types of education which help us to understand the phenomenon of education. They are, for example: Jivan shikshan, Sahaj shikshan, Nivratta shikshan, samavaya shikshan, Nitya Nai Talim.
29) The education in which one cannot identify whether work is being done or education is being imparted is called the samvaya system of education.
30) Education should take place such that the student does not know that he is being educated (samaj shikshan).
31) Education is a fruit.
32) We should develop detachment towards education.
33) Vinoba has said about himself, "one came across many things, but did not find knowledge. After leaving the college, many door of knowledge wide opened."
34) The word teach is a wrong word. The teacher teaches, and the pupil learns is wrong way of saying. The thing that is not given is education. Life itself is an education.
35) The education should be without any examination.
36) The student should be free, self-governing and self-controlled.
37) Kantoombic school means synthesis of life and thinking, industry (udyog) and education.
38) The discrimination in respect of basic industry is advisable.
39) The system in which the poor are served, there is no gap between knowledge and karma, the aim and means both are pure in Nai Talim.
40) Nai Talim means Nitya Nai Talim which creates Nitya new society (samaj).
41) Vanprasthashram is the only ashram for the teacher.
42) Nai Talim is the education of "Also" and not "Only".
43) In Nai Talim, industry (udyoga) has an important place. But to make a suitable person well trained for a given work, or to make clever, a knowledge as ambiguous, or to the means for livelihood, are not the aim of Nai Talim. The aim of Nai Talim is to effect a total development of qualities of the human being. The goal is to bring about the progress of speech, body, intellect, mind, etc.

The Basic Principles of Education

(i) The life and education should not be separated from each other; life and education should not be bifurcated as is done today. Life and education should be given light.

(ii) The humility is born of vidya.
(iii) The students should wake up early in the morning.
(iv) Brahmacharyashram
(v) Veda is the soul of education.
(vi) Education is one that liberates.
(vii) Teachers should not become merely vocational.
(viii) Vedantic emphasizing Advait or unity of life.
(ix) Knowledge resides within individuals.
(x) Education that is imparted according to needs is beneficial
(xi) The concentration of mind is the essence of education
(xii) Self-education
(xiii) Education for all
(xiv) Observance of Brahmacharya
(xv) Components of Education:
- Manual or Physical development
- Intellectual development
- Moral development
- Promoting social service
- Spiritual development
- Artistic development
- *Vyavaharic* development

The theory of "purusharthas" is a foundational theory of Indian civilization, of Gandhian general philosophy or thought, and of educational matters the field of education.

Gandhi-Vinoba philosophy can be stated in the form of a few "equations". These "equations", formulations, sutras, have been mostly constructed by Vinoba. They are:

Life = Pleasure (1) + Sacrifice (2)

Dharma = Four bags: Faith, Truth, Love and Sacrifice.

The letters of Vedas are available in books, their meaning is to be searched in life.

Charity = Equal respect: the most important value.

Vishwa Bhasha (world language) = Love

Vishwadharma = Vedanta

Minimax Life-style = Minimization of wants; maximization of spirituality

Science plus violence = Sarvanash

Science + spirituality = *Sarvodaya*

Hind Swaraj = Vedanta

The essence of all religions = *Satya* (Truth), *Prem* (Love), *Karuna* (Kind)

Sahachitta mesham

Yekchitta, Samanchitta, Sahchitta

Santa Samooha Bamo

Yoga—Sarva shresht Yoga

The theory of purushartha providing a framework within which we can study Indian philosophical thought. Gandhi has reinterpreted this theory, and this interpretation is important for understanding Gandhian thought on education and other fields. The theory of purushartha is the key to Gandhian thought in general and education in particular.

The theory of purushartha posits that a well-lived life requires the co-ordination (harmony) between four purushartha which are called Canonical goals of life. They are:

1) *Dharma* (ethics of duty based on experience)
2) *Artha* (wealth and power)
3) *Kama* (pleasure, both sexual and aesthetic)
4) *Moksha* (spiritual freedom)

Various Ashramas were created during pre-independence and post-independence eras, Gandhi had started the practice of setting Ashramas in South Africa. Vinoba had set up the Ashramas in the recent past. Hundreds of Ashramas are existing in India.

Gandhi-Vinoba philosophy of education is the ethical philosophy. Dialectics of consistency and contraction are all resolved well. The ultimate referent is God and Truth. But between Truth and God, God is more important.

Sometimes, it is argued that Gandhi's philosophy has much in common with Western philosophies which uphold the ideal of a more just and equal society. The doubt is whether the Western Industrial civilization is capable of such vision. Above all else, Gandhi valued self-sufficiency and autonomy. These were vital for his vision of an independent India, Gandhian scheme of education (Nai Talim). The scheme involved the combination of Swaraj and Swadeshi. They highlighted the following aspects of education:

- There is no difference between manual and intellectual (mental) work on the other.
- The work of craftsman, labourer should be the ideal model for the "good life".
- He wanted to free Indian teacher from the interference from outside, particularly, government or state bureaucracy.
- The basic education reduced government interference, and at the same time reduced the dependence of teacher, on the text-books.
- The rationale for text-book debate or text-book issue is as follows: (a) when text-books are mandatory, the living word of the teacher carry little value, (b) when the teacher who teaches from text-books does not impart originality to his pupils, (c) Basic education ends the teacher's subservience to the prescribed text-book. BE scheme presented a concept of learning that simply could not be fully implemented with the help of text-books. (d) BE gave full freedom to teachers to handy matters related to preparing the curriculum. (e) BE denied the state the power to decide what teachers taught.
- Thus, BE gave autonomy to the teacher.
- BE scheme is in the mould of libertarian approach to schooling that transferred power from the State to the teacher.
- Education's central aim is the building of the powers of the human mind and spirit.

A truly Integral Education has three Central Aims: (a) growth of the soul and its powers and possibilities, (b) the preservation, strengthening, and enrichment of the nation soul and its Dharma, and (c) to raise both the individual and nation into powers of the life and ascending mind and soul of humanity. Many of the ideas mentioned above find their equivalents in the Gandhian thought on education. The emphasis on body, heart, mind and spirit in the educational process is the most visible one. Like Aurobindo, Gandhiji has also emphasized the cultivation of heart and the refinement of human emotions and impulses.

Aurobindo has illuminated the nature of new supramental consciousness, the conditions necessary for coming of a new spiritual age, the kind of gnostic being who will be the pioneers of spiritual age, and the nature of transformed social structure in such a spiritualized society.

The education, the Integral Education, plays an important role in bringing about the evolution of man's consciousness and societal conscious. It has been argued by some (Beloo Mehra) that the importance of educational thought of Aurobindo and Mahatma Gandhi is the same, but they appear to be emphasizing different things. Gandhi is deeply concerned with human society as it exists today, while Aurobindo makes us set our eyes on the future spiritualized society.

Is Gandhian philosophy of education integral? Some people feel that it is not integral, but it is holistic. Integral means "poorna" or complete, while holistic means concerning all aspects of existence.

Gandhi was against imitation of Western, English education by India. In fact, he was a strong critique of Western civilization and had rejected it. He has argued that many people do not have an idea of what education is? How it should be valued? And so on. We assess the value of education as we value shares and other commodities in the market. We conclude that girls do not have to do a job, then why should she be educated. Thus, the importance, value of education is decided on the basis of job, employment what one would earn as a result of education. The opposition of Gandhi to Western education was very strong. It is worthwhile to repeat this point. It has been rightly told by some people that no one rejected colonial education as sharply and as completely as Gandhi did. Similarly, no one put forward an alternative as radical as the one he proposed. Gandhi's rejection of Western, modern civilization was all encompassing, he called Western civilization as rotten and "Kingdom of Satan".

Gandhi subjected Platonic, Christian, and Stoic values to great experimentation and reinterpretation. He was a philosopher but not a stoic. The similarity between stoic thinking and Gandhian thinking should be interpreted to show that there was convergence and not influence of stoics on Gandhi. As said elsewhere also Gandhi read a lot, but he did not blindly accept and follow what he had read. He reinterpreted and transformed Ruskh, Tolstoy, sermon on the mount, moral conscience, faith, duties over rights, non-violence or ahimsa, spiritual liberation (Moksha); Anekantwad was accepted by him (Multiple Partial Truths).

Gandhi's asceticism did not spring from Stoics but from early Christians. He talked about "bad thoughts" (undesirable thoughts). Truth, non-violence, *Sarvodaya*, and Sataygraha and their significance constitute Gandhi and his teaching. Contrary to what some people have argued, the Gandhian philosophy (GP) can be concisely stated as "Gandhism". But Gandhiji himself has averred that there is nothing like "Gandhism" which exist anywhere. Once in a long while one finds that the word "Gandhism is used to describe GP. But this is wrong because this term does not honestly, truthfully express what Gandhian thought or GP contains or covers. Long back, it was suggested that we should replace this term by some other better term to avoid continuation of the wrong use of "Gandhism". This however has not happened so far. There has been suggestion that Gandhian way may replace "Gandhism".

While explaining the meaning of education, the following sayings can be very helpful:

- *Dnanam parmam Dyeyam*
- *Vidya vinayen shobhate*
- *Nahi Dnanen Sadrushm pavitrameh vidyate*
- *Vidya saman chakshu*
- *Dnanam Tritiyam Manujasya Netrum*
- *Savidya ya vimuktaye*
- *Sarvasya Lochanm shastram Yasya Nasti Andna Yevam*

That the meaning of knowledge is not without ambiguity is shown by following lines of poetry:

> Where is the knowledge we have lost in information; where is the wisdom we have lost in knowledge?

We need to be alert regarding the correct use of words. At present information is regarded as knowledge. Information technology is designated as knowledge economy.

Gandhi's philosophy and his actions were rooted in his belief in the unity of human life. The core of Gandhi's educational proposals was the introduction of productive handicrafts in the school curriculum. He wanted to make the learning of craft the centre piece of the entire teaching programme. His proposal intended to stand the education system on its head. Gandhi's philosophy sought to make education system financially independent and also politically independent. He wanted to free the people from outside dependence. The right to autonomy of the teacher is in tune with Tolstoy's approach. He wanted to free the teacher from the slavery of the bureaucracy. Till Gandhi pointed out, the job of school teachers was to teach contents of the text-book. Gandhi was not in favour of teachers teaching from the text-books. He would make school teaching with text-books minimum. Why? Gandhi's reply was that if books are treated as vehicles for education, the lively word of teacher, the living word of the teacher has very little value. A teacher who teaches from text books does not impart originality to his pupils.

Gandhi's basic educational plan implied the end of the teacher's subservience to the prescribed text-books and the curriculum. This plan gave to the teacher freedom and authority in respect of the curriculum. It was a liberation plan because it denied the state the power to decide precisely what the teacher may do in the class room. It was a libertarian plan which was in accordance with his wider philosophy of social life and politics. Thus BE implied a dramatic reduction of the state's sphere of authority. This should make clear to us that how Gandhi's even simple ideas were really profound.

Gandhi-Vinoba rejected the view that education should be pursued for its own sake, that it is inherently valuable. They believed that religious dimension is important in the educational processes. Education for them involved both the breadth and depth. When these two are combined, the whole person gets educated, and what is affected is self-realization and preservation of social values. The principles of autonomy and heteronomy are harmonized (Glyn, p. 51). True education has to be religiously oriented and religiously inspired.

One of the most valuable contributions of the BNE would be to keep the state far away from the education in the country, the entry, the growth, interference by the state have played havoc in many cases. The State-independence is a boon to the educational system. Therefore, the economic, political, non-interference, financial autonomy, self-dependence are a very important positive features of the scheme.

Education is life and life is education. The school is an institution at which ideal society is created. Education should prepare home comers into committees, etc. It should enable, facilitate students' knowing of moral and ethical values. Genuine education does not consist of cramming a lot of information.

A school is an institution which is an extension of the home. This is a place where an ideal society is created and the child learns to love to be honest, to be without fuel.

The popular conceptions of power and politics typically reflect the civic education and socialization of citizens, through what is taught at home, and schools, and also the lessons attached to political activities and rituals, elections, and civic commemoration. When this kind of civic education takes hold, it serves to legitimize political power, and so on.

Gandhi believed that in a situation of ignorance and alienation, all laws and systems of Governance are of little value for the people. Further, when education becomes an instrument of dominant groups, with vested interests in it, it loses its capacity to train individuals. The public participation in Swaraj requires that each individual has an unrestrained ethical autonomy.

In 1936 MK Gandhi put forward his own alternative scheme of mass elementary education, known as Basic Education or Nai Talim. His scheme was quite different from the philosophical ideas of both the Romantic tradition and Brahmanical traditions. He emphasized that artisan-apprenticeship skills, manual training, and related discourses should be the central and main basis of all primary and elementary education. He believed that in a largely agrarian poor society, communication and manual skills related to artisan's work and vocational training could be the most profitable form of popular education.

The ultimate goal of education is "freedom from fear". This was a truly radical move. The knowledge of productive handicrafts such as weaving, spinning, leather work, pottery were associated with lower caste groups. Knowledge and skills possessed by them were never considered worthwhile knowledge by upper caste in India. This thinking is still operative in India. It is due to the existence of such understanding that the Basic Education Scheme received extremely critical response. It was not only not adopted, but also condemned. One of the philosophical foundation is that medium of education can be only the "mother tongue". The learning must necessarily be through mother tongue.

What justification one can give for handicrafts in the school system? First, Indian people could not afford to provide education for all children unless the schools could generate some resources from within. Second, the more financially independent the schools were, the more politically independent they would become. It is obvious that political independence means independence.

For analyzing the need for the appropriate education, type of educational system, Vinobaji had discussed what he himself has called "*Paddhti Panchak*" comprising "*Keval Paddhti*", "*Parishesh Paddhti*", "*Samuchaya Paddhti*", "*Sanyojan Paddhti*", and "*Samawaya Paddhti*".

In Sanyojan system, the tenet of knowledge through work is accepted. But the work has only a secondary importance. There is an artificial arrangement here.

In Samwaya system, any craft that has many aspects i.e. craft with multiple dimensions is used along with class-room teaching. The combination of craft and class-room teaching is expected to achieve three things:

(a) It helps to develop all the strengths, capacities of students,
(b) To impart knowledge that is useful in and for life,
(c) To make available the means of livelihood.

The Samawaya system is different from any other existing systems at present, and it is the outcome conclusions arrived at the end. Nai Talim is Samawaya system of education.

We have to impart holistic education. We have to create educational systems which will uplift the body, mind, Atma, intellect, ethics of all. We have to concentrate on our strength for total development of villages. It is to be noted that in order to do this, there is no need for building organized systems.

The results obtained from the transformation just mentioned would be really revolutionary if the following changes in education also occur simultaneously.

- The medium of education should never be English in India. The big expensive building is not necessary.

- Education means an all-round drawing but the best from child and man-body, mind, and soul.
- The man becomes fully human being through education.
- According to Kant, the purpose of education is that our very identity as human being rests on it. 'Man becomes fully human being through education.' E. Kant

Once we know advaitism, it becomes easier to argue that the purpose of true education is to know the self which is akin to knowing the Truth, Gandhian philosophy of education consists of Advait philosophy. Sometimes, a distinction is made between classical (religious) Advaitism, Shankaracharya's Advaitism. It has been argued that Gandhian understanding, interpretation of scriptures shows that Gandhi was nearer to classical advaitism than Shankaracharya's advaitism. (Glyn, 2001, pp. 1-13).

Gandhian thought or Gandhian philosophy is universal and timeless philosophy. According to this, the ideals of Truth and Non-violence are relevant to all human kind. Gandhian philosophy believes that human kind is undergoing gradual moral evolution. Human beings do have the capacity to resolve conflicts non-violently; this might be difficult but not impossible. Gandhian thought was conceived out of action, as a guide to action, and by a man of action.

Gandhi believed that the historic task before human kind to progress towards the creation of a non-violent social, economic order by non-violent struggle. The philosophy of *sarvodaya* resolves all kinds of doubts.

As the foundation of the Gandhian social order is spiritual, political questions are seen from the moral or "humanistic" perspective. The welfare of human beings, not of institutions or systems, is the ultimate consideration. Gandhi-Vinoba philosophy has the following ideals also:

- Decentralization as against centralization in respect of governance, administration, economy, polity, regions, income and wealth, etc.
- The minimization of competition and exploitation in the economy, and encouragement to co-operation, co-existence.
- Production on the basis of need and not greed. Production by masses from mass production.

- To enhance the purity, simplicity, beauty of villages, rural areas; to really bring down on earth the agrarian, Arcadian civilization.

As said before, education is not filling the mind with a lot of facts nor is it the amount of information that is put into your brain. It is the man-making education which we want. Education is the manifestation of perfection that is already in man. We want that education by which character is formed, the strength of mind is increased, and the intellect is expanded. If the poor cannot come to education, we must reach them of the plough, or factory. The prime duty of education is to develop the intellect which the man can harness the nature for the wellbeing. According to Gandhi-Vinoba, the real education is that which expects a total development (samagra vikas) of a person. The true education is that which enables us to know that we are not body or mind.

Gandhiji's Fundamental beliefs on which his educational philosophy is based are:

- Education is life itself.
- The highest aim of education is knowledge of God and self-realization.
- His conception of Nature of Man.
- Hindu philosophy holds that "Maya" leads man to a bondage.
- It is a fate of man to be alienated from his deeper being.
- Manual training is essential for man. It is good for him.
- Education must be self-supporting.
- Education to be universal/must be free.

Gandhi used to talk about property division, to adhere to truth. Truth is a moral tradition; you will have to "charya". Truth itself is a moral law; it bridged the gap between the moral actions. To adhere to truth is based on the principle that truth-based actions are better than those not based on truth. Mere mental adherence to truth is not enough.

One of the unique things about Gandhi-Vinoba's educational philosophy is a very high level importance given to *Vratas*. Vrat chintan, Vrat Upasana, Vrat, Nishta, Vrat Sadhana, Vrat discussion have been given a very high level of dependence. We discuss below this aspect of philosophy of Indian education.

They believed that the best education can be imparted at home and not in schools. But if we must send children to school, our schools must be like our homes. The knowledge at the beginning should be given orally by the teachers. During the first year: (a) no books, (b) no learning of alphabet, (c) no going to school, (d) education at home, (e) if going to school is a must, schools must be like homes, (f) teachers should be like parents of the child, (g) in the first year, children should get education from teachers orally. This is the only arrangement for educating children of the whole of India, no other arrangement can better this arrangement.

In such a way, it implied a programme of social transformation. Gandhi-Vinoba sought to alter the symbolic meaning of education, and to change the established structure of opportunities for education. He wanted schools to be self-supporting. Gandhiji advented handicrafts in school also because he valued that educational institutions must be self-supporting.

Vinoba stressed the value of self-reliance in education. What is self-reliance? Self-reliance has a very profound meaning. The teaching of some handicrafts to students is not enough. Education must be of such a quality that it will train students in intellectual self-reliance and make them independent thinkers. If this were to become the chief aim of learning, the whole process of learning would be transformed. The present school syllabus contains a multiplicity of languages and subjects, and the student feels that he needs the teacher's help for years together.

The first and least part of this self-sufficiency is that the body must be educated and made skilled in a craft. A second and a very important part of this self-sufficiency is the ability to acquire new knowledge for oneself. Freedom implies not only independence of other people but also independence of one's own moods and impulses. The man who is a slave to his senses and cannot keep his impulses under control is neither free nor self-sufficient. Temperance, vows and service have their place in education.

Gandhian philosophy believes that human kind is undergoing gradual moral evolution. The view is that human beings do have the capacity to resolve conflicts non-violently; this might be difficult but not impossible. Gandhian thought was conceived out of action, as a guide to action, and by a man of action.

7

Nai Talim

This Chapter is devoted to the discussion of the origin, evolution, limitations, growth, philosophy, and value system of the Nai Talim which is a potential Alternative Educational System (AES) or educational paradigm. Gandhi-Vinoba were highly dissatisfied with the then prevailing educational system in the work. They conceived, progenited, engendered, pioneered the new system of education, namely, Nai Talim or scheme for Basic Education. Chapter Seven is in a sense an extension of Chapter Six, because both of them discuss the same theme or subject matter, namely, Educational Philosophy of Gandhiji and Vinobaji. In spite of being a revolutionary idea, it is not known much in all strata of society. Therefore, we have devoted much space for its discussion.

What is Nai Talim (NT)? What it is not? Put it simply, Talim means education, training; Nai means new; together, it means new education. Nai Talim is known by some other names also. It could mean educational system which is better than the existing, prevailing educational system. Nai Talim also means Buniyadi education, Basic education, Wardha scheme, Nitya Nayi Talim (NNT); Vinoba-Gandhi System, National or Rashtriya education.

Nai Talim is a life philosophy; it is not creation of merely some rigid, straight-jacket organization or framework. It would be free, independent, autonomous institution. Nai Talim is "Jeevan Darshanam". Its paradigm has global/universal vision; its social organization is the aim of NT. It is radical, revolutionary system.

Nai Talim in Gandhi-Vinoba's vision has the following features as given below:

(1) There would not be any straight-jacket framework or rigid structure of a Nai Talim System.

(2) Nai Talim is closely related to social organization.

(3) "Sharir-parishram nishta" and Samya yoga as Mantra, and root industries (Mool udyog) as its Tantras.

(4) Old Talim (OT) differentiated between mental labour and "body labour". Nai Talim holds that both types of labour have the same value; in fact, Nai Talim tries to integrate the two. Old Talim appreciates capacity, competence, while Nai Talim regards capacity to be the means of equality.

(5) It is time to accept that in education, we do not have to teach history, grammar, maths. We have to teach life.

(6) The facilities for education, preparing text-books should be decentralized, and it will be such as will take into account the endowments of each village. The uniform books are hardly useful in education.

(7) One of the fundamental tenets feed the body by doing intellectual work to do so is not a correct "Dharma". Sharir should be maintained by sharirshram only. This is a "bread labour" tenet of Nai Talim which underlies the roots of Nai Talim.

(8) It must be grasped beyond any doubt that Nai Talim is not a reformed version of any other scheme or plan. it is an independent, free, special, radical, revolutionary idea.

(9) Nai Talim means establishment of new values. Old Talim condemned stealing. Nai Talim condemns accumulation also.

(10) In the regime of Nai Talim, self-dependence and samyayoga are like two lungs and they must be present in Nai Talim.

(11) Nai Talim is not any modified Western scheme, borrowed by us. It is very much an indigenous, free, unique system. It means establishment of new values. In this dispensation, the teacher would be a child; and child would be grown up.

(12) In schools, prayers should be said daily and this should be done in Mother Tongue. Buniyadi Talim means Talim which is given to pupils in the beginning itself. Nai Talim is for everybody in the country. There is no need to think of separate talims for every man and society. Our whole

education would be based on Buniyad of Nai Talim. There is no difference in education for cities and villages. The Nai Talim is viewed as a system, a method, technique. It is a self-controlled system, it is not licentious system. It is like a sea. The various rivers go and meet the ocean; similarly various thoughts may merge in it.

(13) It is the creed of Nai Talim that knowledge and work (Karma) are one, they are not different from each other. When it is not possible to separate unity from duality to say that there is "Samavaya" in such a relationship. The educational system in which Karma and *Dnan* are not distinguished from each other, we say that there is "Samavaya" between Karma and Dnan.

The relationship of Samavaya is expressed by Dhaneshwar in the following Marathi "Abhanga" very well.

"Tuja Saguna Mhanu Ki Nirguna re' |
Saguna Nirguna Eku Govindu re || "

[O'Lord, shall I call you manifest, or shall I call you unmanifest|
Manifest and unmanifest are both Him||or Govinda]

(14) Nai Talim is a plan for giving bliss "Aanand" for 24 hours a day.

(15) Nai Talim seeks to impart free and compulsory education for all boys and girls between the ages of seven and fourteen.

(16) To impart education through some craft or productive work.

(17) To impart self-supporting education.

(18) To impart education through the mother tongue only.

(19) To promote ideal citizenship.

(20) To develop flexible curriculum, and to offer free environment to the students. The subject of the curriculum would be Basic Craft, which may be either spinning and weaving, carpentry, agriculture, fruit and flower cultivation, leather works, cultures, fish, poultry, any handicraft according to the local need, and home science for girls.

(21) Nai Talim removes the barrier between the educated and not educated; between manual work and intellectual work, between the rich and poor, and between the village and town.

(22) Basic education is activity-centered; the child is not a passive learner but an active participant in learning process. It fosters learning by doing.

(23) Basic education is child-centric, and it harnesses constructive and creative instincts of the children.

(24) It is based on the cultural and social heritage of the land. Therefore, it inculcates social and moral values.

(25) It is truly an education for the whole man. It aims at a harmonious development of the body, mind, and soul.

(26) It recognizes the dignity of labour. It inculcates domestic values like co-operation, responsibility, fellow-feeling in students' mind.

(27) The scheme is economically and financially productive, it is based on the principle of work, work occupies a central place in Nai Talim.

(28) The system is capable of removing class and caste distinction. It can bring social solidarity and national integration.

(29) The characteristics of Nai Talim are: Education is for liberation, freedom, sakshatkar, moksha.

(30) Nai Talim talks about predominantly rural education in India; such an education is craft-oriented. The obsessive pursuit of knowledge is to be avoided.

(31) In Nai Talim, spiritualism, socialism, and non-violence would have important place. The intellectual work should not be below 10 per cent per annum. This concept would favour increasing self-reliance and organic growth over speed of development and modernization.

(32) In Nai Talim Curriculum for different ages would be:
   (i) First seven years with stress on physical education.
   (ii) 7 to 14 years for reading, writing, music, etc.
   (iii) 14 to 21 years devoted to learning Arithmetic, Biology, etc.
   (iv) After 20 years of age, politics, religion, psychology, war and peace.

The Nai Talim holds that books are not necessary for teaching/learning at least at the initial stage. The books are not only not necessary but they are harmful also. Gandhi (and Vinoba's) objection to students making the use of books was on moral, ethical, and practical (Vyavaharic) grounds. They were of the view that books are not necessary in the first year itself for learning subjects like geography, history, etc. The students will learn these subjects and poems in "sahaj" way. They should not be required to cram alphabet, numbers, etc.

The Need for Nai Talim

The education at present is not being imparted as per this philosophy. But that will have to be done. When the society tries to introduce and implement the new system of education, the genuine, difficult question, difficult hurdle that would arise concerns the availability of suitably trained teachers. At present, training colleges do not perform this function. Therefore, National Universities will have to accept this responsibility, to take up this task and cause. This is a natural thing which needs to happen. To find out newer and newer ways, strategies, policies which will enrich the education in India is the "Dharma" and privilege of National Universities.

The question that arises while reforming education is how do we introduce and implement education of Gandhiji's conception? As said earlier, the present Government Training Colleges and Rashtriya Vidyapith are not doing their real job. It is the "Dharma" and privilege of these institutions to experiment, according to Gandhian vision.

However, it should be underlined that ultimately we cannot reform Indian educational system on the basis of Government institutions or ideas, measures as discovered by Europe, England, etc. One thing is clear that what goes on in Government schools should be looked at skeptically. The Government education can be harmful to the ideal of "Swaraj" and our culture. Therefore, to take a path opposite to Government education may be more beneficial. Certain features of Indian realities vis-à-vis European realities should clear this point.

(i) The medium of education is English abroad. In India, the medium of education will not be English.
(ii) The educational institutions are expensively built in the West. In India, this will be avoided. Our schools will have simple and less expensive buildings and other infrastructural facilities.
(iii) The knowledge of letters and literature is emphasized. Our education will not emphasize learning letters.

(iv) There, education and religion are separated. In India, we believe that discarding religious education is harmful to the country.

(v) The history that is taught in Government Schools and English schools is distorted, tampered with.

(vi) Economics that is taught in Government schools justifies interpretation in English method.

(vii) Government schools in Europe support, depend on urban culture, while National education supports culture of villages or rural culture in India.

(viii) The teachers in Government Schools do not insist that people should be critical, cultured, and knowledgeable.

As per Gandhian and Vinoba's perspective, one of the tests of good education is what is happening in the country in respect of rural culture, villages civilization, urbanism, etc. In a good educational system, there would be a spread and growth of rural, village perspective and attitudes. The education should help spread ruralization and reduce urbanization, urbanism. For this to happen, the mentality of students in urban areas should favour rural values, rural culture, rural ways of life. In our schools, students, all students from both rural and urban areas, students should be village-life-lovers. All students must take interest in village-life, and all of them must spread over the entire country and engage themselves in the service of villagers.

Gandhi-Vinoba's views on adult education and policy for reducing the size of illiterate population are unconventional. They are inspired by the Indian science of education. They were not as committed as others for devoting resources for adult education which was also called "people's education (*Lokshikshan*)", "Spread of knowledge of alphabets" (*Saksharata Prasar*). They were of the view that while the attention is paid to the branches, the roots are neglected. They held a very "radical thought" on education. They used to say that it is not a matter of worry even if vast number of people does not know the alphabets.

The teacher with grand personality has disappeared now. Today's teacher has become a mere servant. The students do not keep in touch with their teachers in life. There is no "Guru-Bhavana" today. The education does not enjoy freedom, autonomy even as much as judges. In proper arrangements, teacher should be above the judges.

We hear a lot about adult education or people's education (PE) or Lok-Shikshan, literal education. A lot of money is spent on spreading the knowledge of alphabet. The money is spent but the effect is only on branches and not roots. As a result the spread of literal exchange tends to become strength resisters, Gandhi-Vinoba had argued that it is less of an evil if much of the population remains illiterate.

Thus, their position on spread of literacy is clear. Illiteracy will do but the hands must be affected. Therefore, we should not emphasize or give high priority to the programme for spread of literacy. We should not worry about expenses on such a thing. The programme for people's education (*Lok Shikshan*) should be properly examined.

Education through life, and life through education is the moto. Business or commercial-minded teachers should be shunned. Education is the fruit of fulfilling or doing one's duty. We should free ourselves from attachment to education. Today's education is harmful evil. Today teacher-taught mutual feeling (Bhava) does not exist. At present, there is absence of attitude of sacrifice, service, and morality. There is no practice of "*Swadharma*". The free thinking is not regarded valuable. Today's schools destroy the self-soul (*Atmanash*).

Today, the Governments, societies, and individuals fall in the net of bad education. Everybody feels that he is helpless. If it is so, today's schools and colleges should be closed till the gaps are eliminated. The true knowledge is available outside the schools. Today's system of education is altogether unnatural and obstinate. Education must create a natural strong feeling that education is "Ananda". But today, education is regarded as a prison. The education must be natural (*sahaj*). Essentially, man is not evil. The education and teacher must be natural (*sahaj*). Today, teacher is one who does not possess any quality or competence, who is bored by work, lazy person. The true education can be obtained by staying with the ideal teacher. The teacher must become self-realised, self-proved, self-obtained educational centre. The nature is the real, true source of knowledge.

The true knowledge is available outside the school. The colleges offer many things but not knowledge. Leaving the college opens many doors of knowledge. This nation is divided in two parts. In one part, crores of people are doing gross labour, in another part lakhs of students are being given idiotic education. In the nation, two classes (sangakame) and (Kamsange) proliferate.

Today's teachers described in the Vedas are vastly different from each other today, teacher is only a servant. These days, students do not keep in touch with their teachers. The justice department has a greater autonomy, freedom than the education department. This should change and teacher must get greater freedom than what is enjoyed by the judiciary.

The present educational system causes pieces of life. In the first part, 25 years are spent on education without any work, and to live without any education in the next 25 years. Thus life and education are separated from each other. The responsibility of life is not a horrible thing. Even some educationists think that life and education are separate from each other.

Nature and Features of Nai Talim

Nai Talim ought to increase the self-discipline among the students. Nai Talim does not approve that students should live under some artificial discipline. Today's society or today's social organization is artificial, and it is founded on inequality. Therefore, the students who come out of the portals of schools would generally be rebellious, dissenters. Such a student would oppose the society, but this protest would not be gentle, and humble.

Some valuable thoughts on Nai Talim:

(i) It does not accept that the value of body labour should be lower than that of mental labour.

(ii) It does not accept that the differences between body labour and mental labour should create classes in the society.

(iii) In Nai Talim, knowledge and Karma are not separate from each other. This is the spiritual side of Nai Talim.

(iv) All people are socially equal.

Nai Talim or Basic Education scheme had a number of merits, revolutionary in nature. The scheme was an embodiment of the perception of an ideal society. It comprised small, self-reliant communities; and it would have individuals living in small co-operative communities. Basic Education scheme tends to move education from formal towards informal education, which automatically enjoys autonomy and self-regulation. The concept of Basic Education or Nai Talim is concerned with learning that was generated in everyday life. In Basic Education, individual is important but within the principle of cooperation.

Nai Talim has many objectives or aims. A few of them are given below:

(i) To make all villages well-integrated among which there is Advait.
(ii) To end the inequalities in and between villages.
(iii) To make revolution happen i.e. to work for revolution.
(iv) To impart knowledge through work and to establish completely new society or social order. It is necessary to emphasize that the Nai Talim of Gandhi-Vinoba's conception is not some old system which is repaired, which is renovated and called Nai Talim. Basic Education or Nai Talim is educational system which is completely fresh, completely original innovation.
(v) To integrate Nai Talim with Bhoodan, Gramadan. In Nai Talim schools, there would be thinking, experimentation, meditation, learning and teaching of Bhoodana, Gramadana, etc.
(vi) Nai Talim is a model educational system. In Nai Talim, teacher would be student-oriented; student teacher-oriented, both of them knowledge-oriented; and knowledge service-oriented.

Samyayoga and self-reliance are the lungs in education with the effort or exertion. It is to be noted that there are various values of Nai Talim, and, therefore, Nai Talim is meant to bring about change in values. Nai Talim means establishment of new values.

As Vinoba has put it very interestingly, in Nai Talim, the value of body labour and mental labour is equal. The old Talim valued efficiency, Nai Talim makes efficiency the hand-maiden of equality. Old Talim treats Laxmi, Shakti and Sarswati as separate deities, Nai Talim worships humanity and it makes these deities to serve humanity.

Today, there is a confusion about service and power. To change power is not important. To replace power by service is important. Today's confusion is power for service, and service for power.

Nai Talim, conceived by Gandhiji, is an integral part of his own vision of a "good society" of the "India of his dream". His Basic National Education or NT was planned as the basic preparation of Indian children for a new social order totally different from the existing one. Nai Talim was conceived by Gandhiji as "the spearhead of a silent social revolution" or "creative educational revolution". Nai Talim needs to be seen in its true perspective and its importance appreciated for the society of the future.

Gandhiji tried, through his writings and talks, to convey the real sense of education. Where can we be trained for Nai Talim? In home and from mother and father.

A quick glance of all that set of knowledge should be obtained. We provide a small part of it here for the benefit of the public. We present here important aspects of Nai Talim which is called by many names: (1) Gandhi-Vinoba (Vinoba-Gandhi), educational system, (2) Rashtriya (National) educational system.

Let us briefly note the Nature, Vicharas, Values of Nai Talim In Vinoba's style, let us note "Tantra" and "Mantra" of Nai Talim. What would be the Nature of books prepared in Nai Talim system? These books would be produced after a great deal of "adhyan", "adhyapan", "experiments, experience, and practice". In Nai Talim there would be a confluence of the farmer, and contemplation. Who is the ideal of teachers in Nai Talim. It is the Shri Krishna who is the ideal of Nai Talim teacher. Krishna is called "Jagadguru"; it is the unique side of Krishna that he integrated "Karmayoga" and "dnanyoga". He increased the work, industry, labour, and philosophy. He gave and increased the status, respect to the service worship of the cow. Krishna made the social work the spiritual work.

- Education does not mean information gathering, it does not even mean getting readymade knowledge; it is capacity building within oneself for getting knowledge.
- It is necessary and it is also possible to have higher learning and research in the villages itself. We should have colleges and universities in Taluks, and in District places. As we make progress, we can have colleges at villages themselves.
- In Nai Talim, there would be scope for "*guru seva*" by the students, "students seva by the teachers", social service and Ishwar seva by the Gurus.
- Nai Talim should result in making him "*Vrat snatak*", and not keep him only snatak.

- In ideal school, food science, health science, khadi, and "atmadnan" should be available. Nai Talim has the responsibility to make children self-controlled, strong; only skillfulness is not enough. The students must become *"Hasta-sanyat"*; *"Pad-sanyat"*; and *"vacha-sanyat"*.
- Nai Talim is one self-controlling thought in which mind, body, intellect, etc. should be controlled.
- In Nai Talim, education is given by first, the mother, then the father, then the Acharya. The educational organization is not fixed, inflexible arrangement. It is the responsibility of Nai Talim not to make children good only in speaking; they should also become strong (*Viryavan*).
- Buniyadi education must result in Indian tradition of giving importance to obtain *vidya* and Avidya.
- Nai Talim should not be under the control of the Government. It should be people-dependent.
- The village teacher would be the servant of (sevak) of the village.

Gandhiji wanted education to be free and compulsory for all boys and girls between the ages of 7 to 14 years. The scheme is in harmony with the culture and civilization of India, and which would sort the problems of mass education in a practical way.

The basic idea of this scheme is to impart education through some craft or productive work. The craft and other physical work helps the child to acquire sensor and motor co-ordination, and to appreciate the value of honest labour. The method of training the mind through village handicraft from the beginning as the central focus would promote the real disciplined development of the mind, the advantages of making craft as the centre of education. Psychologically, it relieves the child from the tyranny of a purely academic and theoretical instruction.

Buniyadi education and Nai Talim are more or less the same concepts. The goal of BE is to equip village boys and send them to villages for working as ideal models for the villagers. The inspiration behind this scheme or plan has come from villagers. Thus, BE is for villages and from villages. Today, primary education has become a big joke because little thought has been given to the needs, resources etc. of villages. In fact, today's primary education has completely neglected the life of both rural and urban areas. Buniyadi talim joins or connects all rural and urban boys to all superior and stable principles. The aims of BT are: (i) To develop the physical, intellectual, and moral aspects of children, (ii) To make the whole education self-sufficient, (iii) To make good use of hands.

According to Gandhi-Vinoba, the higher education has harmed rather than helped the enlightenment.

Nai Talim aims at total (*Samagra*) education for total development of the pupil. It would be udyoga centered. In NT, the beginning of the education of the child can be brought about through handicraft, artisanship (dastakari).

Nai Talim is an educational system which was useful and relevant in the past and it remains so now, and it will remain so in future also. There should be clarity about the structure of NT. Manu has said that when the son becomes 16-year old, father should treat him as a friend. The implication of this is two-fold. One, the son should take up the responsibility of life after he becomes 16-year old. Two, the parents and society should take up the responsibility of son till 16 years of age.

Nai Talim originated in Tolstoy Farm in Durban in South Africa. Basically, Nai Talim is a case for "education at home", a disciplined home education which is far superior to school education. Its premise is that changes in the life of parents influence children significantly. Another principle (Usool) of education is that the teacher should never hide his ignorance from the students. Another important point in this context is that books have a very little role to play in education; the teacher should act as a text-book. The talim of body, mind, and spirit's financial self-sufficiency is the operative principle of NT.

Basic Education (BE) or Nai Talim (NT) occupies a unique place in the field of elementary education in India. It is the first attempt to develop an indigenous scheme of education. As a rationalist leader, he had realized that the British system of education could not serve the interests of India. At Round Table conference in London in 1931, he highlighted how the British system was ineffective, and how the literacy rate was alarmingly low in British India, telling the audience how British rule was responsible for this sorry state of affairs in respect of mass education. He naturally arrived at the concept and scheme of BE to promote mass education.

Gandhi's proposal for universal, compulsory basic education

takes the requirements of villages, rural areas, farmers into account. Basic education can be said to be the first major attempt to give rural orientation to the education in place of urban orientation. This approach is in keeping with Gandhi's attention to the masses, the last man, the poor. Just as we used to talk of production for masses in place of mass production, we can talk of education for the masses in place of education for the urban rich.

Would Nai Talim include Religious education? This is an important question but the word religion has been used in a very narrow sense. Therefore, some people say that in order to avoid trouble, it is better not to teach or keep pets at home. But Gandhi-Vinoba position on this point is different. Good character, faith in God, Atma is different from body. Therefore, religious teaching ought to be an important part of Nai Talim curriculum.

The best authentic way to know about Nai Talim is to see Vinoba's views, exegesis, explanations about Nai Talim. He believed that when the political regime changes, the National Flag changes. Similarly, when the regime changes, educational system also should change. In keeping with his belief, he prepared a new educational system in 1937 to be implemented after India became free or swaraj.

Nai Talim may mean "New education" or it may mean "good education" Vinoba used to call Nai Talim as "Nitya Nài Talim" (NNT). Now, NNT means Talim which was yesterday, but which is not today; and Talim which is today may not be tomorrow. In other words, "Nitya Nai Talim" is one which changes continuously on the basis of daily experiences.

A few people with imagination and insight welcomed Gandhi's educational revolution, from the beginning, but most of the educationists voiced doubts. The two kinds of doubts were voiced: (1) First, it was pointed out that Gandhiji's revolution would mean neglect of literacy and literary education. It was also feared by some that work schools would prove to be sweet shops. Gandhiji used all forms, means, the press, conferences, seminars for debating with the skeptics. He was seething with ideas to make educational revolution a real one, and he engaged with critics open heartedly. Gandhiji got a new, important opportunity to discuss a very large number of aspects of education with other scholars in a formal way. The reference here is the National Education Conference (NEC) which took place on October 22-29, 1937. This conference was organized by Marwari Educational Society at Wardha, whose President was Jamnalal Bajaj. The conference was organized to celebrate Silver Jubilee of Marwari Educational Society (MES) and its High School (Nava Bharat Vidyalaya). The Secretary of the Society was Shree Sriman Narayan.

The conference passed the following resolutions:

(a) Free and compulsory education must be provided for seven years on a nation-wide scale.
(b) The medium of instruction should not be English.
(c) The process of education must involve some productive manual work.

The resolutions were adopted as a national education policy.

The Basic Education Conference appointed a Committee under the Chairmanship of Dr. Zakir Hussain, and this Committee completed its work by December 2, 1937 (i.e. in 40 days). The Committee's draft report was discussed by the Indian National Congress in February 1938, and INC accepted the Wardha Scheme as its official policy for educational reconstruction.

The performance/success/failure of the scheme was determined by various factors: (i) Which Party was in power generally, (ii) The abnormal conditions like war-time created difficulties in implementation.

In April 1941, the second National Basic Education Committee met at Delhi at the invitation of Dr. Zakir Hussain. The important aspects of Nai Talim which were particularly discussed at this conference were: Place of Arts in Education; the place of work in education. This 1941 conference was full of life and promise. But the political upheavals like 1942 Quit India movement required Gandhiji's attention to political issues resulting in some neglect of the question of Basic Education. As Ms. Sykes has put it, the next two years were dark, but the darkness preceded a new dawn.

During 1942-1944, Gandhiji arrived at the position that health and education involved the whole men and the whole of society, and therefore, he regarded them as a key to village regeneration and key to gram swaraj.

In January, 1945, "Hindustani Talimi Sanga" brought together teachers from all over the country to confer with Gandhiji still more revolutionary educational ideas. Gandhiji, in his opening speech, stressed on the ideas such as "complete or poorna swadeshi", "poorna swaraj". Unfortunately, the teachers attending the conference did not realize the importance of his views.

Thereafter, the Seventh All-India Nai Talim Conference was held in 1951. The Golden Jubilee of the Basic Education movement was held in October 1987.

This bare sketch of evolution of Nai Talim should give the reader at least some feel of the importance and relevance of Nai Talim. It remains one of the most important contributory subjects to achieve the world-goal of "swaraj".

The several states had adopted the Nai Talim scheme before India gained her independence itself. The several schools were set up specifically to carry out the Agenda of Nai Talim. Yet, today the overwhelming population would announce the verdict that Nai Talim is dead. It would not be possible to find out even a handful of schools which are being run as per the Nai Talim philosophy.

- Paradise is lost, paradise must be regained.
- Co-operation has failed, but co-operation must succeed.
- New education (Nai Talim) has been forgotten, but it must be resurrected.

The 1973 conference passed the following resolutions:

(a) Free and compulsory education should be provided for seven years.
(b) Mother tongue should be the medium of instruction.
(c) The process of education should center around some form of manual and productive work.

Merits of Nai Talim

(a) Economically, the scheme will increase the productive capacity of workers and will also enable them to utilize their leisure optimally.
(b) The knowledge imparted through Nai Talim would be related to life.
(c) The BE or Wardha scheme would be self-supporting in two senses: one, education would be self-supporting in later life, and two, education in itself be self-supporting. If the craft chosen for education is efficiently harnessed, it would enable the school to pay the cost of salaries of

teachers. It would ensure modest and honest livelihood for the student after leaving the school.

(d) Why should education be imparted through mother tongue? Because the proper teaching of the mother tongue is the foundation of all education. Without the capacity to read, write and speak effectively in mother tongue, no one can develop precision of thought and clarity of ideas in other languages.

(e) The BE scheme is financially sound.

(f) It is also economically productive.

(g) It can promote social solidarity and national integration.

(h) BE removes all types of distinctions.

(i) BE is activity-centered education. The child is not a passive learner; it is active participant in the educational process.

(j) There is learning by doing.

(k) BE is child-centric. It primarily considers the constructive and creative instincts of children.

(l) It is truly an education for the whole man. It inculcates social and moral values in the minds of students; it aims at balanced development of body, mind and soul. It inculcates democratic values.

Nai Talim is the Talim which is different from the educational system installed in India by Mccauley, Moolodyoga education. The meaning of "Nai" in Nai Talim means that education which helps to make New Society regularly. Another way of defining Nai Talim is to say that Nai Talim is educational system which has newer and newer aims or objectives.

Nai Talim is also called as Buniyadi Talim (BT) and Buniyadi Talim means that Talim which is given to children from the beginning to the end in the country. To repeat, Buniyadi Talim means the talim which is imparted in the country from the beginning to the end. The "Tantra" of BT (NT) is Moolodyoga, and its "mantra" is physical nature orientation.

Nai Talim has a literal meaning, and also the implicit meaning. In the thinking of Gandhi-Vinoba, the implicit meaning was more important than the literal meaning. The education under Basic Education scheme would be free and compulsory. The important merit of Basic education is that it was expected to cater to the needs of (Indian) society. The village is the pivot, centre, the basic unit of organization of any activity in G-V paradigm. The Basic Education scheme also had rural orientation. It is the conditions in villages which had given birth to the BE scheme. While designing the BE scheme for India, Gandhi and Vinoba's concern was more for village children who were poor and did not have access to educational facilities. In G-V paradigm, BE means to transform village children into model villages. In this context, we should be clear about the terms "basic" and "Nai". The scheme may be designated as basic because it is based on the ancient Indian culture, and it lays down the minimum education which every child is entitled to receive without any distinction of class, creed etc. The term "Nai" is related to basic needs and the interests of the child, and makes use of his basic, innate potential for creative productive work.

In the beginning Gandhiji introduced his new scheme / plan and this plan had come to be widely known as Buniyadi education, and this scheme was for children of 7 to 14 years of age.

After some time this plan was extended to "Poorva Buniyadi" (1 to 7 years of age) and "Uttar Buniyadi" (14 years of age and above). These three ladders of education constituted the "New Education" or "Nai Talim ".

The best commentary, explanation, exegesis of Nai Talim has been by Vinoba. For him self-dependence, self-reliance (Swavalambam) is one of the greatest virtues of man. The other name for Nai Talim is self-reliance. Now, Vinoba has deepened the meaning of this term. According to him, there are three meanings of self-reliance: (i) one should not depend on others for daily food. (ii) For getting knowledge independent power should be awakened, and self-existent (self-born), awareness (consciousness), wisdom (Pradnya) be endowed to pupils, and (iii) man should get enough strength for self-control. In Vinoba's view, *vidya* is for freedom (Mukti), self-reliance is Mukti. What follows is that Nai Talim is self-reliance and Mukti.

Education → Self-reliance → Freedom (Mukti)

Strictly speaking, the basic thought of education and knowledge is eternal. Even then from time to time it becomes dull. It then comes in different form in different ages. This process lends newness to that thought. Accordingly, Gandhi-Vinoba put forth the old, ancient educational thought in India. Ancient educational science and today's needs were combined by them, and a new mixture of thought on education has been put forth before the Indian people that thing is Nai Talim.

Vinoba holds that there are five systems of education known as "Padhati Panchak" (five systems).

- A very important aspect of education in India has been the utter humility of the Guru or Rishi. At the end of 12 years of education Guru used to say to the pupil that he had learnt some *vidya* from him but do not regard me the final word, or authority. You regard only truth to be the last word. Do not use my actions or my words as the authority (Yani asmakam sucharitani tani twayo pasyani, itrani).
- Education is not a business. It should never become a business. It is an incidental or contingent fruit of performance of our daily, regular duty (kartavya karma). The education is the best education which is free from illusion, free from education-illusion "Shikshan-Moha".
- Gandhi-Vinoba have given a very important place to labour, manual labour, sharir shram. That it has been made a part of twelve *vratas* indicating its value in education.

Gandhiji himself regarded Nai Talim as his best and last gift to the nation. And yet, the people have refused to do anything to implement the idea/scheme. The consequence has been the educational crisis although the solution to the crisis was at hand. The objective of Nai Talim is to resurrect the people's interests and to renew their interests in the implementation of the scheme.

Nai Talim has originated from the special Indian tradition and culture. Its essence namely, education through work is not to be found in any other system. Today when mechanization is spreading fast in every field, the education through basic handicrafts has a tremendous utility and relevance and appropriateness. To teach students, to develop them by depending on the atmosphere, conditions surrounding him are the established tenet of Nai Talim. Similarly, Nai Talim cannot be different for villages and cities.

An outline of the scheme of Basic Education:

(a) The basic craft from spinning and weaving, carpentry, agriculture, fruit and vegetable gardening, leather work, and any other craft.

(b) Mother tongue as the foundation of all education.
(c) Total duration of elementary education—seven years (7 years).
(d) Distribution of work in the curriculum:

Item/activity/subject	*Daily time to be devoted*
(i) The basic craft	3 hours 20 minutes
(ii) Music, Drawing and arithmetic	40 minutes
(iii) Mother tongue	40 minutes
(iv) Social studies and General Science	30 minutes
(v) Physical Training	10 minutes
(vi) Recess	10 minutes
Total (daily)	**5 hours 30 minutes**
Total (in a year)	**228 days**

Limitations, Shortcomings of Basic Education or Nai Talim

Like other contributions of Gandhi, this idea of Basic Education (BE) also has been severely criticized by certain scholars. On further thinking, it would be found that a lot of misunderstanding, dogmatism underlies the criticism.

(i) It has been said that BE idea is based on unsound psychological foundation. Human Nature has three aspects—cognitive, affective, and conative. BE emphasizes the last aspect but ignores the first.
(ii) It is impossible to establish any natural association between craft and all the subjects of cultural values. It is absurd to hang all knowledge to the peg of a single craft.
(iii) Education suited to our national genius would have definite religious basis. Craft-centered education is decidedly alien to our ancient ideals. (N.B. This is one of the most unconvincing criticism. Religious, moral, ethical values, Indian tradition and culture have influenced MKG greatly.)
(iv) BE is not suited to industrialized social order or an age of industrialization. This criticism springs from the static and not dynamic set up. A new educational system will be working in changing levels of industrialism.
(v) The scheme will introduce too much of a ruinous competition.
(vi) The insensitive approach by intellectuals has led them to heap certain epithets and condemn the philosophy of Nai

Talim. For example, BE is a fraud which is being committed on the nation by those who are in power.

(vii) It is a sort of political stunt to play with the sentiments of the people.

(viii) BE is a fallacy. The very fundamentals are wrong.

(ix) BE is a farce. It is impracticable.

(x) BE is a fad. It has no sound psychological and pedalogical basis.

Why has Nai Talim not given results? This scheme of education has not produced any tangible far-reaching results. Although the new scheme has many merits, (it contacts Gandhi's penetrating vision, it cuts all the fruitless verbiage discussions) it could not revolutionize the Indian Educational system. In fact, the initial response of the people was highly discouraging, disheartening. The scheme of Nai Talim was first published in Harijan in 1937 in the form of articles. When these articles were first published, there was a storm of protests in educational circles. People who had worked in the seclusion of their offices and files were thrown off their balance. These ideas were opposed and dubbed as entirely impractical. The system in India then and now also has been more and more book-centered, it did not help to develop intellect, emotions, and character.

The sub-committee of the 1937 conference was in favour of a broad liberal curriculum for elementary education and expansion of facilities for technical education. Financial responsibility for compulsory primary education was assigned to be that of the state.

In contrast to Gandhi's utopia of village republics enjoying considerable autonomy, the modernist utopia featured a strong centralized state responsible for building an industrial infrastructure in order to ensure a high standard of living for all. Nehru agreed with the main pedagogical assumptions underlying basic education, namely, a craft or manual activity stimulates the child's mind.

Now, it may be remembered that all responses to Nai Talim were not hostile. Many eminent educationists welcomed the idea of BE, and many extensive plans to implement such ideas were prepared. Despite the range in the interpretations that the Nai Talim proposal, the scheme of basic schools was implemented on the considerable scale in several parts of India after independence. However, the implementation of BE scheme could not survive the "development decade" of 1960s when the Indian economy and its politics entered into the phase featuring centralization of power, and so on.

Moral Dimension of BE Scheme

Gandhiji never endorsed the separation of young children from their parents for studies or any other reasons. He believed that the education which the child imbibes in a well-ordered household is impossible to obtain in hostels. The widespread easy availability of the system of crèches signify choosing wrong path.

The children undergo their most formative part of their life in the first six years of their life. About 80 per cent of their mental make-up takes place by six years of age. Gandhi believed that for proper upbringing of children, the parents ought to have a general knowledge of the care and nursing of babies. In fact, one view puts it that the development of the child begins in the conception stage of the foetus itself.

The decline, fall, the failure of Nai Talim occurred because we allowed the Governmentalization of Nai Talim to take place. We should have created the pure models of Nai Talim at various places, but we, instead worked through different Talimi Sanghs.

It is well-known that Vinoba has often extended, enriched the meaning, scope of words, ideas, etc. One example of this is the name given by him to the Basic education. The widely known and widely used name is "Nai Talim". Vinoba changed it to "Nitya Nai Talim" (NNT).

Nai Talim is a life-philosophy. It is not only one super-structure for education. In life we daily get new, fresh experiences, and we need (should) to change our life daily on the basis of those experiences. It must be noted that Nai Talim cannot be introduced by keeping today's social structure intact. It is not possible to introduce Nai Talim by keeping the present social system as it was. It is not an arrangement for creating regime of "equal pay for equal work".

Nai Talim is costly and dependent on others. The change of values has not taken place as required. The elected, honest, hard-working teachers are conspicuous by absence. Teachers have become politicized and politicians. Those who were to oversee education have themselves become power seekers. Teachers themselves do not have faith in education. The flag off revolution is not in the hands of teachers as it was expected to be.

It has been argued that in Nai Talim schools, students have to do manual labour, physical work.

The present critique, educational system had been set up by the Britishers in the early 19th century in India. It came to be criticized during the freedom struggle. Many eminent Indians, political leaders, social reformers and others had protested against the system. But no one rejected colonial education system as sharply, and as completely as Gandhiji did. He wanted to use this project to make British Raj weaker and weaker.

In order to persuade the opponents, Gandhiji wrote at length on various aspects of education, and in India of 1937, every sentence he wrote contained a revolution. He changed the meaning of education. What is education and what it is not? For him education meant an all-round drawing out the best in child and man-body, mind and spirit. Literacy in itself is not education. He argued that education is not literacy; literacy is not the end or beginning of education. He told that literacy in itself is not the highest development of the mind and soul.

At this juncture, an opportunity arose which gave him leisure to work on education. In and around 1937, he constantly posed the problem of financing education in the form of conflict between prohibition and education. He said, "the cruelest irony of the new reforms ... lies in the fact that we are left with the liquor revenue to fall back upon, in order to give our children education. In short, from the very beginning, he was against using tax revenue for education. Gandhiji faced a lot of severe criticism and opposition to his thought. In order to meet this opposition, he wrote his seminal article in "Harijan" of the 31 July 1937.

The sudden death of Mahatma in 1948, his idea of (BNE) came to halt. Although National Education Commission was set up in 1938, and it prepared a Report on education in India, there is no doubt that Gandhi's approach received a great setback to efforts to create educational system in India on Gandhian lines. In pre-independence era, provincial Governments had tried to implement the scheme. The teacher's training schools were opened to train teachers for the implementation of the scheme.

The scheme was officially accepted by the Congress. After Gandhi's death, the scheme was buried quietly never to be revived so far.

8

Educational Revolution through Acharyakul

So far we have discussed how Indian educational system (IES) was during the ancient, Buddhist, and Islamic periods. The said discussion was meant to serve as a background to the current discussion. The present chapter discusses a very original idea of Acharyakul. The triangle of education has students, teachers, and administrators as its three sides. The quality of education materially hinges on the quality of teachers. The exploration of ideas and means to enhance the excellence in teachers, therefore, is an important task before all the educationists in the world. The idea of Acharyakul is totally original, revolutionary, and inspirational; it has a tremendous potential for transforming education in the world. It was conceived by Vinobaji and put forth by him for the first time on March 8, 1968.

The Origin and Meaning of Acharyakul

During the 1960s, the state of education in general, and teachers as well as students in particular had become extremely worrisome in India. Dr. Zakir Hussain, the then president of India had met Vinobaji to discuss how to meet this crisis. Around this time, Mr. Karpoori Thakur, the then education minister of the Bihar State also met Vinobaji to seek his guidance to tackle various problem which were plaguing the Indian education. As a follow up, Mr. Thakur took the initiative and organized the Conference of all Vice-Chancellors of all Universities in Bihar, Principals and teachers in all the Colleges in Bihar in December 1967 at the stopover of Vinobaji who was on his Padyatra for Bhoodan and Gramadana.

Mr. Triguna Sen (the then education minister of India), Jayaprakash Narayan, and others also participated in the said Conference. Vinobaji blessed the Conference and guided the participants in respect of various dimensions of Indian education with a focus on the teachers. He advised that an organization or a formal body of all teachers in the country should be set up to do the work relating education and other issues on a continuous basis. He gave the name "Acharyakul" to this body. He had said, "that the establishment of *Acharyakul* is an important event for us. The reservation was about its name. I do not expect to find out a better name than Acharyakul. It is a beautiful word. It fits well in Arabic also. It reminds us of all teachers in the world. Its another beauty is that it is a familial (*Parivaric*) word.

The Nature and Philosophy of Acharyakul

The word Acharyakul has two distinct parts: Acharya and Kul which are "artha-ghana" or "dense in meaning". Acharya means a male or female teacher. All the pre-primary, primary, secondary, and the university and college teachers are acharyas. Vinobaji has said that all those who have a faith, trust in the "Vichar-Shakti", "Shabd-Shakti" all those who have capacity, power of thinking are Acharyas. Therefore, scientists, technologists, professionals like accountants, lawyers, judges, journalists, literary persons, artists are also eligible to be member of Acharyakul.

In ancient India, many people used to live in the forest to meditate and they would wander from door to door to pass on the truths they had discovered. The word Acharya has "char" "dhatu" root in it and it conveys that the man must practise what he preaches. The acharyas were characterized by practice of "Achar, Vichar, Vichar-prachar-Sanchar". Today's teacher is far cry from "Acharyas" of the olden past. One of the aims of *Acharyakul* was to effect the "Gun vikas" of the present day teachers.

The word Acharya is ancient and it used to be used for addressing sages like Shanker, Ramanujam. It has been used for Vinoba, Kripalani, Bhagavat and so on. These acharyas used to be highly respected, revered, even worshiped. There might have been some fakeness some times in all such traditions. This can be seen in the way all the Acharyas were treated. Even the Kings and other powerful people used to bow to them; "His Highness" used to bow before Guru. The teachers were addressed as Guru, Guruji, Sadguru, Guru Mawooli, Guru deva, etc.

There is a verse in Sanskrit which equates "Guru" with "Parbrahma".

> *Gurur Brahma Gurur Vishnu*
> *Gururdev Maheshwar* I
> *Guru Sakshat Parabrahma*
> *Tasmai Shri Guruve Namha* I I

It is certainly true that all the teachers today do not have all qualities, but, it is expected that teachers should aim at towards this description. The picture here is the picture of the ideal teacher, and all the teachers are expected to attain, achieve this ideal.

The Acharya Kul is a "Sangh" or "Sanghatan" of teachers. But Vinoba has used a different word for the proposed organization of teachers. We had Buddhist sanghas in India. We have "Sarva Seva Sangh", we have "Rashtriya Swayamsevak Sangh", we have unions of labour; we have Federation of Teachers Associations. Vinoba did not find that either the Sangha or the Association, or the Union or the Sanghatan as the appropriate name for the proposed organization of teachers. He found that the appropriate name for the said organization would be the "Kul". In the field of social organizations, it is perhaps for the first time that the name of "Kul" has been used. It is a "familial name", "Pariwarik" title.

The Acharyakul is to work for multiple Revolutions. It is expected to revolutionize the personal lives of its members through their efforts towards "Gunvikas". It is expected to revolutionize the universe of education. Similarly, it is expected to revolutionize the social-political-spiritual life at the national and international levels. In other words, Acharyakul is expected to obtain a solution to the crisis of survival of man, society, and planet. The Acharyakul would work towards elimination of inequality, social, economic, political inequality, injustice and exploitation, and so on. So far, we had always thought of either the labour or the farmers, as the vanguard of revolutions. It is after a long time, after 1917 revolution that Acharyakul is being thought of as the vanguard of total revolution. The uniqueness of this revolution lies in the fact that for the first time, revolution would be a spiritual revolution.

The working of Acharyakul would be expected to help the people to develop, nurture certain values, certain "Gunas" in their personal lives. The teachers would, by and by, become real acharyas because they would be practising what they would be teaching/

preaching. Acharyakul would make its members "*Sant Samuha*" i.e. group of saints.

The withering away of the State, the Statelessness i.e., "*Shasan-Mukti*" has remained an important goal of socio-economic-political revolution in India. But such a goal has remained unachieved so far. The redeeming way to achieve the said goal is not the governance of the nation-State but the discipline (*Anushasan*) of the Acharyakul.

According to Vinoba, Acharyakul is a spiritual organization. He had great faith in Acharyas, he wanted them to be free, and if they became free, they can generate great power and strength. If the Government opposes Acharyakul, its members can use the technique of satyagrah. He expected them to come forward, exert for eliminating their own bad qualities, nurse and nurture their own good qualities bring about their "Gun-Vikas" and then guide the people. The strength of Acharyas is redeeming, inspiring, and complementary, their status is very high and it should remain high. Acharyas should realise, they should know that their status is even higher than that of the Government. Their brain should be high and their heart should be large. The state of India at present is very miserable, and next to Government, it is so because of failure of Acharyas. Vinoba has gone to the extent of saying that the sorry state of India today is first due to Acharyas, the responsibility for failure rests on Acharyas more than on the Government. The Acharyas should exert to be "Unmanas" (i.e. to lift oneself above the mind). Acharyas should not remain confined to their class rooms and educational places; they should come out and work for establishing peace in the world. The Government can suppress the peacelessness (Ashanti) but it cannot extinguish, quench the condition of peacelessness. That is the job of Acharyakul.

In short, Vinoba has put the responsibility for "Ashanti" on Acharyas. He has said that the moral responsibility for the extinction of Ashanti and establishment of peace in the world is that of Acharyas. How? The best weapon for establishing peace is education, and that weapon is with the Acharyas. *Acharyakul* can, thus, bring happiness and peace in our life. If we want to save the world, Acharyas discipline is the only means for achieving this. It should be clarified here that generally Gandhi-Vinoba were not believers in institutions or organizations. Then how he has advised the people to create Acharya Kul? One may say that this is not a very significant objection. Acharyakul is a family: parivar, biradiri. It is a large organization; it is not a very strict, hierarchical body; it has freedom, autonomy, openness, equality are all embedded in it.

Many people are critical of such a unique, original idea on the ground that it is unimplementable; it is nice but impractical. Where are the Acharya of the vintage of Shankaracharya, Ramanujacharya and others? Today's most of the acharyas do not possess the qualities indicated by Vinoba. How many teachers are *Nirbhaya* (fearless), *Nirvair* (enemyless) and *Nispaksha* (partyless). They are expected to shun the politics, but they are immersed in politics. Someone has said that if you want to see the real politics, do not go to party headquarters, go to colleges and universities. Elevating the minds, agitationless, peacefulness are not even known to many teachers. Acharyakul would not have any inequality of caste, creed, etc. Those who do not believe in the power of thought cannot become a member of *Acharyakul*. The self-examination or self-probing is the necessary activity of the members of *Acharyakul*. It is meant to increase the freedom, autonomy of teachers. The *Acharyakul* is expected to rouse the power of teachers and to harness it for the good of people. To repeat, Acharyakul is not an institution, it is a "parivar". Vinoba has given the following agenda for Acharyakul. Pursuit of knowledge, purification of one's own chitta, to be affectionate towards students, doing something continuously for the development of students, to contemplate neutrally on the social issues and problems, and those decisions which have been arrived at and neutrally, unanimously, to be conveyed to the students and others concerned; to guide the society, to be on right path, to solve the problems, difficulties by non-violent means.

One of the aims of *Acharyakul* is to recognize the strength of teachers, to rouse, or to wake up and to make it functional, and to increase or develop it further. Acharyakul would enhance the autonomy of teachers to decide curriculum, teaching methods; the decision in all these aspects can be finally taken by the teachers only. The parivar of acharyas would be straightforward, simple (saral) and not complex; its organization should be loose but its loyalties should be strong.

In India, Gandhi and Vinoba have launched a revolution which is unprecedented; it seeks to effect in India a change (parivartan) in mind, heart, thought, conditions, etc. This revolution or "abhiyan" is to be known as Swaraj or Gramswaraj, Hind Swaraj or *Sarvodaya,* or Gramdana. It is expected that Acharyakul should provide leadership to this revolution. It is the responsibility of teachers to guide mankind as to how man should behave as man with man and give new values to the society. Acharyakul should dissuade the youth from favouring violent means, it should teach the youth to engage in constructive work, to teach students to balance the enthusiasm and discriminative ability—all these are the duties of teachers. Today teachers have forgotten their own strengths, capacities, status (haisiyat); they have also forgotten their duties. The Acharyakul is being established to wake up the teachers and remind them their duties; it is to remind them about their moral strength and moral duties.

The aim of *Acharyakul* is to create ideal teachers, and ideal education system. The students would understand the meaning of self-control, discriminative power if they see that they are being taught by their teacher from their own experience. The teacher should become a gardener and not a rein. The educational plan should be such in which teacher would be attached to students, the students should be attached to teacher, and both teacher and student should be attached to knowledge and service. Mahadevi Varma has explained the nature of Acharyakul very well. According to her, it is an institution for contemplation, or prediction for achieving mental emancipation. The job of the teacher is to join the youth's enthusiasm with the discriminatory power of the elderly, and thereby to develop the creative capacity of the students. Our difficulties, problems of today are those of teachers and not of students. The teachers have created unions or associations but the purpose of them has been mundane, selfish, narrow. Acharyakul is an organization which is completely different in the process of formation, its methods, and goals. The aim of Acharyakul is to inspire the people for self-churning and self-purification. The teacher is expected to maintain the higher status of the citizens and society through their mental ability and penance.

Certain principles and tenets of our civilization are eternal, they are ancient, and they have been handed them over to us. It is our duty to keep them secure and develop them. Every member of Acharyakul should take a vow and burn like a lamp; then only they can light the society. Their guiding principle is "Atmadeep Bhava". One of the important works for Acharyakul is to decide as to what should be the philosophy of education in India.

Sarvodaya and Acharyakul

One of the points Vinoba has talked innumerable times in any and every place is to ask teachers, students, social workers, and ordinary citizens to shun politics like a plastic, because it invariably, always breaks, never joins. He would want that every member of Acharyakul should follow it scrupulously.

The ship of *Sarvodaya* and the boat of Acharyakul invariably tend to flounder on the rock of effectiveness or practicability. What should we do if the public is not convinced by us? Vinoba's answer has been to increase our "Tapasya" or i.e. penance or self-purificatory action. Also, the word-power (shabda-shakti), may be inadequate, which is due to inadequate "Tapasya". There may also be low capacity to convince others. Similarly, we may be unconvincing because our own conduct does not reflect our thinking, there is a great hiatus between our Achar and Vichar (self-conduct and thinking). In other words, when we face a predicament of the type mentioned above, we should do what Saint Tukaram, Christ, Shankaracharya did. (a) Tukaram said, "Words are our only weapons", (b) Christ has said, "We should use the weapon of 'forgiveness' till the end", (c) Shankaracharya has said, "if people do not listen to us once, we should explain again and again. I have only this weapon with me."

The idea (Sankalpana) of Acharyakul is one of the very last ideas which Vinoba has bequeathed to us. Acharya means Guru, Guruji, teacher, "Master", Sir, etc. Acharya Kul is an ancient, Vaidic idea. We used to have "gurukul" in the past. There are certain differences and certain similarities between Gurukul and Acharyakul. Both relate to education. Acharya is the centre in both. Acharyas in both are realized persons. But, the aim, organizations in them differed. India has a long tradition of Acharyas starting from Shukracharya, Dronacharya, Guru Vashist, Sundipany to Vinoba, Atre, Kripalani to Rajnish, Bhagawat.

The Indian culture/civilization has celebrated teacher in various ways. One comes across the reference to importance of "Guru" or "Guru Mahatmya" Patanjali has seen God in "Gururupt" i.e. in the form of Guru. The Indian civilization has seen Rishi, Muni, Yogi, mother, father in the form of Guru.

As said earlier that we call Guru as a "Gurumawooli". We have already quoted the verse in which Guru is seen in the form of Brahma, Vishnu, Mahesh, etc. There are "Gurupanthi" groups or communities in our tradition. We talk of "Gurudeva". All this discussion is meant to show that the status, power of teachers is very high indeed. The analysis implies the Godly status of Guru. Shikhas worship Guru. It is expected that teacher should be tri-gunatmak; he should not participate in politics; he should have a feeling of love and affection towards children; he should be "Adhyansheel", chintansheel, etc.

The aim of formation of Acharyakul is not to agitate, struggle, fight, strike for concessions, special privileges, pecuniary benefits, and other mundane considerations. The aim is to rouse, wake up the teachers as the protectors of human values. The teacher is the pivot of educational systems. According to H.G. Wells, "the teacher is the real maker of history. The teachers have a great responsibility of moulding the personality of the students. The teacher can change the society and bring about social revolution. Let it be recalled that Vinoba, like H.G. Wells, had said that revolutions can be made by the teachers alone.

The ideal teacher is a highly exalted being. The members of Acharyakul can find inspiration from ancient Gurus. Acharyakul is a family, spiritual "biradari" of teachers which may bring about multiple revolutions. In Indian tradition, Guru is "poornehu", complete in himself; he imparts the highest vision of Vedanta to his disciples so that he may fulfill himself also. The reading of writings on Gurus or Acharyas would reveal that, the qualities which are attached to the Gurus are so exaggerated that some readers may be put off, and they may find themselves convinced that Acharyakul is an impractical idea. On this point, one may say that while some of the qualities were actually possessed by certain Acharyas, the others were the ideal to be emulated by any teacher.

Since the issue of practicability is important, let us dwell on it a little more. How should be the teacher? Independent, thinker, perseverant, discriminating, fearless, enemyless, partyless, attached to students, attached to society, attached to knowledge. He imparts liberating spiritual knowledge. The Guru is nothing but pure consciousness, absolute bliss, eternal wisdom. The whole affair is strictly not impractical because we have the precedent that the Indian civilization which is regarded the best civilization has been constructed by the Acharyas only. There has been an exalted tradition of Acharyas, which made Bharat in ancient times. If earlier acharyas could do it, why the existing acharyas cannot do it? The use of Sanghshakti has been favoured.

Acharyakul: Nitty-Gritty Dimension

Membership

(i) From the beginning to University level, all teachers can be the members of Acharyakul.

(ii) Those teachers of people, literary people, journalists, thinkers, and social servants who have faith in the loyalties of Acharyakul can become members of Acharyakul.

(iii) For becoming a member of Acharyakul, the following Resolves will have to be made:

- (a) Power, party-politics, and groupism will be shunned.
- (b) Non-violence will replace violence as a method, and change of heart, and power of thought will be adopted as the means.
- (c) One will have to do some work of education of the people, service of the people, and creation of people's power.
- (d) Duties are more important than rights.
- (e) To donate at least one paisa daily for the working of Acharyakul.

Organization

(a) Acharya Kul is an autonomous organization of the teachers, and it can decide the policy about its relationship with other organizations.

(b) The basic unit of Acharyakul would be any institution from primary school to university. The members of these units will elect the presidents or conveners of these units.

(c) The units within a prakhanda will create a local Acharya Kula.

(d) The decisions of elections and the decisions of committees will be taken on the basis of consent of all.

(e) The period of office-bearers and committees would be for one year but a person can be reelected more than once.

(f) The use of funds collected through membership fee would be broadly as follows: 5 per cent for central Acharyakul; 10 per cent for local Acharyakuls; 85 per cent Janpadiya Acharyakul.

The Scope of Work

(a) To organize meetings and conferences (councils) for autonomy of education.

(b) To publish the journal—organ of Acharyakul and literature of Saints for inducing the habit of study and teaching (Adhyan and adhyapan) among all.

(c) To organize meetings and councils (conferences) at the national and international levels for solving the intellectual, social, national problems and to arrive at Acharyakul's solution.

(d) The service of the people (Lokseva), people's education (Lok shikshan), increasing people's power (Lokshakti Nirman) and people's policies (Lokniti)—to work for these things. Acharyakul would work for "Loksatta", "Lok Niti", "Lok Manyata", "Lokshakti", "Lokseva", "Lokrangh".

(e) To work for unhappy students and teachers.

Aims of Acharyakul

(i) The aim of Acharyakul is not to get some benefits or concessions or privileges. It is to ensure that teachers as a body wake up to their duties as a protector of human values. The Acharyakul works towards teachers, work for change in social values.

(ii) To work to keep education autonomous, like the judiciary.

(iii) To see to it that the agitation is in the surrounding areas is eliminated with the help of education and not by violence.

(iv) To remain aloof from party politics.

(v) Not to become a member of any political party.

The teaching is some "Vrat", it is not a vocation. I regard body-worship of secondary importance, but regard aim-worship of primary importance. I am a friend of all those who are staying in my country. I am a knower of elements (truth) and a guide to the people. I am a worshiper of the power of knowledge and the power of Dharma. To make man is my aim. I would remain aloof from selfish power-attached, party-attached politics. The teachers should have four attachments:

> Labour-attachment, Knowledge-attachment, Students-attachment, and Social-attachment.

9

Gandhi and Vinoba on Students and Teachers

The philosophy of education of Gandhi-Vinoba has been discussed so far by taking up various sub-themes of education such as the fundamental principles, the inadequacies of the present educational system, New Education (or Nai Talim), etc. There are various parts, aspects, constituents, stake holders in education. The teachers and students are the most important constituents, and the discussion of philosophy of teachers and students would go a long way in understanding the whole philosophy of education (PoE). Both Gandhiji and Vinobaji were the teachers and the students in their whole life time. Of course, in one place Vinobaji has said that he was more a student than a teacher in his life.

Both Gandhiji and Vinobaji were in continuous dialogue with each other and also with other teachers and students. They have given a large number of suggestions, instructions, injunctions, and advice to the teachers and students. All those discussions are part of overall PoE.

We give below certain events, points of tete-tete between Gandhiji and Vinobaji on the one hand and students and teachers on the other. There is no doubt that students are the focal point of the educational system, the student becomes student because of a teacher. As we have shown in the chapter on Acharyakul, the teacher has an exalted status in the system of education. The teacher had such an exalted status because of his work (his karma). Vinoba has quoted the following "Vedic sloka" to express teacher's unique role:

> *"Twam no asya amterut kshudho*
> *Abhishasterau sprudhi*
> *Twam na uti tav dhiya*
> *Shiksha shachishat gatu vit"*
>
> [Hey! Gatuvit, hey powerful path finder, our ignorance, our hunger, and our diseases may please be destroyed. Give us the best education. Your intellects, power, productivity and other powers be opened up.]

With the passage of years, the decline in the status of teacher has occurred and today the teacher has become just a salaried or a paid worker. The following pen picture of today's teacher describes quite fittingly, quite accurately the lowered position of the teacher.

Today's teacher is the one who does not have any competence or excellence to do anything important for life, who has lost capacity to do important work, who is bored by anything that is worthwhile, who is boastful of possessing only the knowledge of teaching, who is buried in books and who is a lazy being.

The objective of teacher should not be to give, to pass on some or other information; their task is to create, to teach student as to how to get or obtain knowledge independently.

In education, students' and teachers' goals should be such as to lead to "prajna" or self-born, and it does not surrender to diseases, emotions, excitement (vikaras), or to be overpowered by "vikaras" is to use freedom, independence, and self-reliance. Vinoba has emphasized the following duties, and responsibilities: Freedom to have independent thinking (or chintan). With faith (Shraddha), one would not feel fettered. Today's students do not understand the significance of "Mukta chintan" (free contemplation). Students must have faith, independence and so on. But, unfortunately, students do not understand very well these important things. They form Unions, if anybody has a right to complete or "Poorna" freedom, it is the students who should have it. It is not possible to obtain knowledge without faith and buddhi (intellect). "Vidya" and Shraddha are the same. The faith is the beginning of knowledge; knowledge ends in intellect.

Thus, Vinoba has continued, students should never lose their freedom to think. The teacher should never force the students in any respect, if he does so, he is not a teacher. The one who gives intellectual freedom is a true teacher.

The conditions in the world today are extremely worrisome as per Vinoba. He has warned the students that today under the name (pretext) of discipline, the students' freedom is being compromised; the student brains are being mechanized. Although discipline is necessary, under its name, everywhere mechanization is impacting the students' brains.

It follows that the Department of Education of the State should not be under the control of the State. This ought to be changed. The students should neither form Unions nor they should surrender their freedom. Vinoba dreamt of making student a "sant" (saint). Another duty of students is to gain control over the self. Who is "sant"? The one who makes "satya sankalpa" (vow of satya) is sant, and the students are expected to be saints.

The third duty of students is that he should become service-oriented; he should always be engaged in some or other service (seva).

The next duty of students is to be always alert about things taking place around them; he should abandon low loyalties, should become universal being (Vishwa Manuesh) so as to minimize conflicts and peace is maintained.

A study of writings of Gandhi-Vinoba would yield the following valuable advice to the teachers and students:

- The teachers should take the responsibility of life on their shoulder just as the farmer does. The educational structure should be designed such as to involve students also in responsible tasks.
- To stay with the ideal teacher itself is a good education. The teacher is a self-realized educational centre and to live in its proximity itself is to get education.
- One of the things which has adversely affected Indian education is too many or plethora of holidays/vacations.
- There should not be any holiday, vacation for the schools and other educational institutions. If holiday has to be given, it should be in rainy season. There should not be even a one-day holiday in Nai Talim schools. If there is a bliss in obtaining knowledge, why there should be a holiday at all?
- The teacher in the school should also be a servant of the village. The village school would be a service-centre. The

school children and teachers will help the villagers in whatever service they need.

- The whole of our revolutionary work depends on the teacher in the village. The teachers in (Nai Talim) schools would be the most studious (Adhyansheel), and the teacher should always be ready with the solutions for solving any problem the villages would face.
- In the schools, we should be in a position to nurse, promote "faith in Truth" "Satyanishta". If I am "Satyanishta", I will always have faith in others. Even if I am not able to make others "*Satyanishta*", I must remain so.

The important principle of education is that we should not thrust, forcibly include knowledge in the students; instead we have to create a craving, a strong desire for knowledge, and also create a necessary strength, capacity for obtaining knowledge.

Students need to cultivate the strength, capacity for a good memory as well as forgetfulness. The important thing in education for both the students and teachers is knowledge and ignorance, *Vidya* and Avidya.

In one of the chapters of compilation, Gandhiji has given some injunctions for the teachers and students, the two most important entities in education.

- Gandhiji has impressed upon the students to know and live according to his "dharma". Without "dharma" there can be no knowledge, wealth, health; the life will be barren in the absence of "dharma"; there can be no progress.
- Should students take part in politics? Yes, if by politics we mean the science. But if it means political action, it is dangerous to enter politics.
- Students should also respect the elders because disrespect to elders leads to the ruin of community. Further, students should serve their country. The value of one's learning is judged not by "what you know" intellectually but by "how you act".
- According to Gandhi, students they should live life as Sanyasis observing Brahmacharya. Students should cultivate faith in God. They should shun intoxicants. He has illustrated how to do public service during vacations as follows:

(i) Conduct night and day schools with just a short course.
(ii) Visit Harijan quarters, clean them.
(iii) Take Harijan children on excursion, sight-seeing, picnics, historical visits, etc.
(iv) Reading to them Ramayan and Mahabharat.
(v) Teaching children simple Bhajans.
(vi) Taking medical aid to ailing Harijans.

- Like Harijans, the service needs to be rendered to caste Hindus, and the students should do this also. The education must educate children to be humble, they should pay for their own education; they should learn the value of self-study and manual work. Indian students need not go abroad in large number for education there. They should participate actively in the work initiated by social workers about educational reconstruction. As a part of this, MKG asked to improve teaching methods, build National Education, cultivate the spirit of sacrifice. The students in India must become makers of New India. They should develop positive outlook.
- It is the task of teachers to make teaching absorbing. The teachers need to cultivate or build heart to establish heart to heart contact with the students. We need educationists with originality, fixed with true zeal for educational revolution in India.
- Teacher is a mother. She who cannot take the place of mother can never become a teacher. To fulfil this as far as possible, the man-teachers will have to acquire the noble status of a mother.
- The brother-and-sister relationship is the only proper relationship between boys and girls studying together. There should also be a relationship of mutual affection, mutual trust between the teacher-students. Gandhiji has advised the teachers and students to keep on striving till the one improves as a human being.
- It is interesting to know that Gandhiji was aware of the problem of relationship between the girl and the boy students having co-education. Gandhiji believed that just as brother and sister cannot have a husband-wife relationship; the teacher-student relationship also can

never become husband-wife relationship. This has been called a "golden rule" which serves as guarantee for the protection of girls from their teachers.

It is again a revolutionary thought that in life we should be a student of students. The teacher must learn more and more from his students. A true teacher regards himself as a student of his students. Anyone who does not learn from his students is a worthless person.

Thus, Gandhi-Vinoba had put teacher in a very high, exalted, honoured position. But this unique position of the teacher declined and reached lower and lower depth. The teacher was a great "path finder", or "path discovered" or an inventor or entrepreneur. India or Bharat is the making of Indian teacher. The teacher should be compassionate (Karunavan), with character (shilwan) and clean intelligence "pradnyavan".

In olden days, intelligent, wise, persons used to be called (Pradnya Purushaha) who used to run the educational institutions, and they had complete independence while doing so. The teachers were expected to be the vanguards (Agradoot) of peaceful non-violent revolution.

Vinoba has told us as to what kind of interrelationship between teachers and students existed in the past and what kind of interrelationship should exist?

- The teachers should love their pupils, they should have attachment, and affection for students who should be called "students should be Devo Bhava".
- The teachers should always be engaged in study. If students have faith in anything, it is the knowledge or Dnyan. Teachers should have faith in spreading of knowledge, power of knowledge, and sea of knowledge. When Guru and Shishya think, reflect, meditate, and practise together, the humanity gets the experience-born or experience-based knowledge.
- When churning of thinking takes place and it combines with experiments, it is called Nai Talim.
- Teachers should be neutral. They possess immense power,

[N.B.: The "shloka" and a "poem" given above have been reproduced here from Vinoba, book on *Shikshan-Vichar*] spiritual power (Adhikar), and their status is very high—all this be realized by the students. The teachers' work is superior (Shreshtha). The students are the most valuable wealth of the country. The students get the knowledge of the "sansar", guidance, *vidya* from the teachers. They have "teacher-Dharma", and they must live by that "dharma".

- As stated above, the status, power of teachers has declined and today the status of teacher has become like that of the bullock and the maid servant or paid employee, etc. The teachers and students must remain under shock.

In India, there has been a wonderful practice or tradition according to which the student never fails. Therefore, the position has been that if the student fails, it is the Guru who should be punished. The philosophy has been that "Shishyoparadha Gurur dandaha".

- The three symptoms of Acharya are: "Sheelvan", "Prajnavan", and "Karunavan". Acharya has all three "gunas", and acharyas have made a country like Bharat. In earlier days, teachers were called "Acharyas" i.e. the practitioner or "Acharvan". While leading a model life, Acharyas alone had (have) the capacity to make the public "Acharan". The Indian nation has been built-up through the exertion, efforts, hard work. The herculean task of building the Nation would require again the acharyas; in the absence of such Acharyas it is not possible to rebuild the Nation.
- From ancient to middle-ages, a strong tradition of Acharyas was very much extant in India, and it prepared the society, and it made Vidyadan. When this was happening, the State power (Rajsatta) came and destroyed duly. The India has not been made by rajasatta, she has been made by Acharyas, Santas, Fakir, and Acharyas.
- Among the Ashramas, the teachers should be mainly belonging to "Vanprasthashram".
- Student should learn the art of forgetting as well as remembering. To forget is of a great values; ignorance also can be a bliss.
- Today, there are moves to mechanize students, to make a part of some machine. This trend ought to be halted; the

students have to become "*Sant*" and not "*panth*". Sant is one who is the worshipper of "Truth" or "Satya".

- There are four important responsibilities or duties: (i) To keep our brain independent, (ii) To effect a self-control, (iii) The students should remain service (seva) oriented, (iv) The students should always be alert and keep secured. Today's education is making students convenience-oriented, superficial "Sukha" or happiness. This is wrong and not healthy. Mahabharat has asked the question, "Sukharthinaha Kuto vidya, kuto vidyarthinha sukham".
- Teachers and students, and also others should have faith in those who have faith in "Jnani".
- The line of perennial contact, touch, interaction should always be existing between the teachers, students, and others.
- There is generally no reason for most of the students for going abroad for higher education. Today's craze for going abroad is not desirable, is not understandable.
- According to Gandhi-Vinoba, no one should be unwilling or reluctant to become a student of a student. This is a deep philosophical truth. It is a great lesson in humility. This philosophy may help us to become soft in nature. This suggests that corporal punishment should be avoided in education. We are taught to develop motherly love.

Gandhi-Vinoba has given many suggestions to the students for utilizing their vacations and increasing productivity. Some of them are:

- Conduct night and day schools with just a short course, well-conceived, to last of the vacation.
- Visit Harijan quarters and clean them, taking the assistance of Harijan if they want it.
- Taking Harijan children for excursions, showing them sights near the village and teaching them how to study nature, and generally interesting them in their surrounding giving them by the way a working knowledge of geography and history.
- Reading to them simple stories from the Ramayana and the Mahabharata.
- Teaching them simple Bhajans.

- Cleaning the Harijan boys of all the dirt that they would find about their person giving both the grownups and the children simple lessons in hygiene.
- Taking a detailed census in selected areas of the conditions of the Harijans.
- Taking medical aid to the ailing Harijans. This is but a sample of what is possible among the Harijans.

Vinobaji's suggestions for how to study well are practically useful also. They are:

(1) Instead of studying long-hours without attention and concentration, it is better to study seriously and in a state of Samadhi for a short-time. Samadhi is a main principle in study (Adhyayan).
(2) We cannot get knowledge without studying in a state of "Samadhi". Adhyayan should not be big grossly; gross "Adhyayan" leads to wasting of resources. Man can develop his capacity through serious study.
(3) The life's marga (way) is decided by two dots: (a) Where is one, and (b) Where does one have to go?
(4) In life there is a place for "Karma Yoga".
(5) In short, serious study has the following "Sutra". Small does (Alpa Matre), continuity, Samadhi, karma and definite direction.
(6) Every day, minimum one hour full physical labour has to be conducted.
(7) During vacations or holiday, students should go to nearby villages for making them clean. In general, they should do the "seva-karya" in villages.
(8) Students should decide that they would make friendship with those belonging to others than self.
(9) Students should learn Hindi very well.

10

Towards New Education or Nai Talim

In this chapter we discuss what can be done, what is required, so that new education (Alternative Educational System) can be actualized in coming few years. We present the examples of institutions which will have to be a part of Nai Talim. Similarly, we discuss various pre-requisites for introducing Nai Talim.

(1) Sankrant in Education

Education is a means of all-round progress of man. The pathway to human development goes through education. Education is the basis of achieving one's purpose in life. The prime aim of education is to make man self-dependent (Swavalambi) skillful, efficient, and "Atmasakshatkari" or "Atmabodhi" or "Atmajnani". The word "Sankrant" has been coined by Vinobaji, and it means total revolution in wider sense of the term.

The question that arises is whether any and every system of education is in a position to impart such education? The experiences show that there are many educational arrangements and philosophies which offer maleducation or bad, harmful education. One finds that in the vast number of existing systems of education, only a very few systems meet the requirements of a redeeming system. In fact, as we referred to the crisis in education, the education domain is sickly and needs to be repaired, reformed. Nay, we in fact, need nothing less than a revolution, kranti, and "Sankranti", to use the terms which Vinoba has used with such a great felicity. And in order to effect them, guide them, we need "Krantdarshi" of Ishavasya Upnishad. What is Sankranti? The change at the roots (Moolbhoot parivartan), stable change, samyaksamgra parivartan are required for Sankranti. Similarly, purity of means and goals, are essential ingredients of Sankranti.

The revolution in education needs "Krantdarshi" (in fact Sankranti darshi) for leading the revolution, for being the vanguard of the revolution. The thought on education or "Shikshan vichar" of many ancient and modern sages in India have performed this role. The Indian scriptures have many such wise people, Adarsh purush, Patanjali, stithpradnya, kavi, manishi are but only a few examples.

To this line (ancient and present) belong two contemporary sages, namely, Mahatma Gandhi and Vinoba Bhave. They have given the educational thought which can bring about "educational" "Sankranti". The nature, philosophy institutional superstructure, value system, institutional and ideational prerequisites, as suggested by Gandhi-Vinoba and others are discussed hereafter.

Now, we would explain what types of schools and other educational institutions, what types of curricula, stages of education, what types of ideas, concepts are necessary for replacing the extant educational paradigm by the Alternate system of education or by the model of new education.

(1) Family School (Kautoombic Pathshala)

It is often said that the growth of human brain is more or less complete by the age of five years. Vinoba has argued that our thoughts and our lives should be related, the relationship of thought with life (jivan) should not break. If this relationship (Nata) breaks, the thought tends to become life-less. In today's education, the organization of education is exactly like this. Man lives in the house (home), and gets education in the school. Though it is not realized, this leads to educational sickness and it leads to the gap between thinking and living in life. What then is to be done? The answer is that we should end the separation between home and school; they should be integrated.

The houses of teachers should be made the foundation of education, and above this the superstructure or building of education is the "Family School". Vinobaji has given a number of suggestions about the life-process of the Family School. They are given below:

- The essence of life is the faith in God. Therefore, the daily prayer in the morning and evening should be a compulsory part of activities of the school. This prayer should be all-religious, all-community, "Samuhik" prayers. The policy (Niti) should be "enmity towards none", (Sarvesham avirodhen).

- The purity of diet and purity of "chitta" are interrelated, and therefore "satvik Aahar" is a must.
- To prepare food is an essential part of education, to be able to prepare food is an important part of self-reliance.
- Family schools ought to clean their own lavatories. This will achieve a number of things: (a) elimination of untouchability, (b) end the hatred for any socially useful work, (c) This will impart a really good practical education or training in keeping the things clean. At present a lot of propaganda is being made about public cleanliness. The persons from the top to bottom showing that they value cleanliness greatly. Gandhi-Vinoba had made this a live issue long time ago.
- "Kautoombic pathshala" will not deny any one the access to that school. In such school, there would not be any segregation while sitting for taking meals i.e. there would not be any "Panktibhed".
- In such schools, the habit of taking bath in the early morning should be prescribed. Bath should be taken with cold water only.
- Instead of bookish education, the industrial education for three hours daily must be given importance and space. The Vedic injunction is that only after doing one's own "Karma", of Vedas should be done. After doing three hours' work daily, there is no need for doing physical exercise.
- Spinning must be made a regular and punctual daily work like "National Dharma" and prayer. In addition to the three-hour industrial work, at least half an hour be devoted for the spinning. Takali is a very useful instrument. Everybody must know spinning on Takali for clothing, Khadi alone should be used.
- We should not remain awake at night for any work except service to the sick, etc.
- One should not take meals after sun-set (at night). To implement this rule is important from the point of view of health, arrangement, and Ahimsa.

(2) Daily One-Hour School

One of the most innovative ideas Vinoba has introduced is that of daily one-hour schools. The idea is that these schools should be in villages. These schools would run in the villages in the morning, and they should not be dependent on the Government. Thus, Vinoba has recommended that we should have pathashala which would be Grameen school, it should work in the morning, and it should run only for an hour or so (This can be called valuable Pathashala). Those who are aged less than 15 years would enter the one-hour morning school. The curriculum in the one-hour pathashala would not be much different. In Maha Vidyalaya, the curriculum would include hearing, speaking, Bhajan, Aaradhana. The time of small children sitting for 5/5 hours do nothing, thus wasting their time. Sometimes one comes with a suggestion that schools should be twelve-hour schools. If Gandhi-Vinoba philosophy of education is correct; there is no case for 12-hour schools.

(3) Education for 24-hour Ananda or Bliss

The Gandhi-Vinoba alternative in education differs from conventional or present system of education in respect of the most important aspect of education, namely, the goal of education. While Gandhi-Vinoba education philosophy, like the ancient Indian education, is about nothing less than bliss, Ananda, Sukh, Sachidananda. In Schools the essential nature of Brahma, or the "Swarupa" of the God should be manifest in the whole activity in the school. The school means "Bhakti marg", it means whatever is done in the school, it should be for Ananda. The ultimate goal of education is "Ananda". Thus, the entire programme, activities, Karma of education is for Ananda.

(4) Educational System for Rural Areas and Urban Areas

While designing the alternative educational system, it is necessary that we should make the difference between the rural areas and urban areas. For industrialized advanced nations perhaps we need not do so because urban-rural dichotomy, rural-urban divide is not significant. For a country like India which has a prominent rural-urban differentials, it would be an error to treat its economies as homogenous.

The new educational system should recognize the reality in rural areas, and it should explicitly serve the interests of the rural areas. The education of common, mass of people should be rural, grameen life-style. The educational system should help villages to progress. In such a system, those who live in cities should have concern for the rural people. There should be good level of co-operation among the villagers. It is to be noted that the education for villages and urban areas should not be altogether different from each other, it should be different but it should not be very much different. The educational system should be appropriately different, but it should not be conflicting with each other. There is a basic unity, "Samya" in life. According to him, those who live in cities should be oriented towards villages (Gramonmukh). The rural areas should be worshipper of Nature, they and villages would live with great cooperation.

(5) University in Every Village

One of the suggestions has been that there should be a university or Vidyapitha in each village. Each village should have completed, total education (sampoorna education). The rationale behind this approach is that every village represents a universe, and entire universe happens to be present in each village howsoever small it is.

It is an error to think that the university in a village cannot sustain. Each village has its Nature; it has its history, social knowledge, ethics; co-operative spirit—all such knowledge can easily sustain a village University. Gandhi-Vinoba have solved the problem of small size of each village university by developing the philosophy of "Gramswaraj" in which the unit of activity is a group of villages and not a single village.

The village university idea can be made workable, concrete if the villagers increase the devotion, faith of the people in the village.

(6) The Revival of Sanyasashram and Yati Dharma

The idea of having university in each village can be actually implemented because of existence of novel and unique socio-economic organization in India since ages. The reference here is Varnashrama System according to which the life of the individual was divided in four parts called "Ashramas" namely. Brahmacharya, Grihastha, Vanprastha, and Sanyas; the society was similarly divided into four "varnas", namely, Brahmin, Kshatriya, Vaishya, and Shudra. The main work of each of these divisions was well-defined. For our purpose, one of them namely "Sanyasa-shram" can make one village—one University idea quite workable, feasible, implementable. Suppose, there is a village in which no one in the village can get any particular or a special knowledge. The requirement can be met through a Sanyasi when he visits that village as a part of his itinerary.

In India, there existed a plan called "*Parivrajak Sanyasi*" plan whose "Dharma" was to roam and teach the people. Sanyasi was a kind of "walking university". Thus, it is really great that our thinkers have provided ideas which have made things interactive. Therefore, we have to activate the system of Sanyasi and thereby carry out certain educational reforms.

(7) Education through Labour (Shrama) or Sharir

There can be a new method of imparting education to children. The boys who are needy, poor, should be called and asked to do some or other work. While doing their work, they are given some education also. They are also paid wages for their work. In this arrangement, the boys are said to be given work and not education. Yet while they work, certain things are taught to them. After a point, while earning money, those children would also receive some education. This can be called "learning through earning".

The ideal school would evolve if certain things are done, and certain other things are not done. The science of diet should be taught to all, we should develop sight of knowledge or "dnyan-drishti", science of excreta; science of health; khadi-vidya, and synthesis of science and spirituality, our schools should be clean and decorated.

(8) Manusmriti says "Prapte shodshe varshe putre mitruvad acharet"

One meaning of this advice is that children must take the responsibility of the household once they become 16 years old. Which is the best (Samarth) education? It is the one which makes children feel that life is not a burden, it is worth living. The society must organize education in such a way that children would come to feel that life is not a burden, it is a favour. The above-given Manu's words also mean that the family or the society should not put responsibility on children till they become 16-years old.

Vinoba has clearly given an advice in the form of a "sutra": 'The education of self-dependent till the age of 16, and after 16 years of age, self-reliant education.'

(9) Grameen Vishwa Vidyalaya (Rural University)

What is the meaning of Grameen Vishwa Vidyalaya (GVV)? It is the place where life is "Sarvanga poorna" complete in all aspects.

To repeat, where the life is complete in all respects or aspects is Rural University. There would be a library well-equipped with necessary books. The people would be given land, instruments and implements, houses. The teachers and taught there will be self-dependent or self-reliant. The logic behind RU (Rural University) is that India is a country of villages, and these villages ought to receive good education, the RU was conceived as a plan, an idea, scheme to provide the necessary means for imparting education to the people in those villages. The population in these organizations would be "optimum" or limited. The people in these places would know one another by name. The village is a place where there is an all-integrative habitat; it is also a place where all types of productive activities, professions exist. In order to build "model villages" or "Aadarsha villages", Gandhi-Vinoba conceived that there would be a university in each village. For establishing these new rural village universities, each village, i.e., all the people in each village would choose a suitable appropriate person as a Vice-Chancellor of rural University. This VC need not be much educated (if he is educated, all the better). But he should know well the village surroundings, he should know how to bring about development of his village area; he should have leadership qualities, he should remain neutral politically. He should be a staunch votary of truth and non-violence; and he should become a servant of the village. It should be his aim that his village should become self-dependent and self-reliant. He should discuss all the matters with "gram mandal" and they should prepare a development plan for the village. The teachers in this village-university should be chosen by the VC. In this Vidyapitha, there should not be quarrels, enmity over salary, PF, gratuity, pay-scales etc. His main purpose should be to make his area self-reliant in all aspects. The suitability of teachers should be decided in the similar way as that of VC. All teachers must be self-reliant and those who like physical labour.

All the boys and girls aged 12-18 years would be the students of this University. There would not be any fixed curriculum, nor there any examination, test, etc. The working hours of university would be for 11 hours (from sunrise to sunset). The work to be done in a day would be divided as follows:

- Production, Livelihood: 4 hours
- Language study, Maths, Science: 1 hour
- Hobbies, and provision for future: 1 hour
- Sports and Arts: 2 hours
- Spiritual activity (shravan, etc.): one hour
- Interval period (free): 2 hours

All holidays would be decided by the VC. It is better to sum up discussion on Grameen Vidyapith in Vinoba's words: The idea of Grameen Vishwa Vidyalaya has come up out of need. The blue-print or model of this educational innovation has not been made as yet. But we can say that urban universities and grameen universities should be very similar to each other because in important and first matters, and about life, there can be hardly any difference between the two. Therefore, there cannot be different universities for rural and urban areas.

Buniyadi education must be Buniyadi from beginning to the end. From this viewpoint, the nature of Village University should be such that it will also give all conveniences like urban Universities. At certain stage, they will have to be told that now you will not get anything from the government. Then onwards, they will have to live co-operative life, they will be asked to live a total (samagra) life, and both together should produce a model of urban universities. In such universities, there will be discussions, experiments; their results would be put before the public. However, the real, main thing would be that learners, and teachers both will be self-sufficient, they will work with their hands, they will earn their bread not somehow but in the best manner.

We had referred earlier to Manu's rule which lays down how to interact with sons when they become 16-years old. On the basis of experience of thousands of years, Manu has said that till completion of 14 years, 7-year educational plan is called Nai Talim.

The RU would be full of students because even the poor children would be able to seek admission to R.V. These village Vishwavidyalayas will discuss various matters, they would experiment, and both the teachers with the taught would be self-reliant, they would work with their hands, and they would earn their own living.

Vinoba used to talk about Vishwa Vidyalaya in every village. This did not mean that complete study of all the subjects would be done in each village. What can be done in the best manner or way in the villages would be done in villages, the rest will be done by the cities. There is enough scope for doing great and wonderful things in both villages and in cities. If in every village, people live from birth to death, if all things, all activities are taking place in villages, why is it that we cannot make all arrangements for complete education of the children in villages. The hierarchy in making arrangements for education is a wrong thing to do. The lower (common) education in villages, higher than that in the district, still higher than that in a very big city is a wrong arrangement of education. To repeat, if from birth to death everything takes place in the village, village Vishwa-Vidyalaya in rural areas can impart that much higher education as required.

Can village vishwavidyalaya provide facilities for education in science, technology, and also for research? Vinoba's answer is a definite "Yes". Even today, all universities do not offer all facilities and subject for teaching and research. In the same way rural universities can offer specialization depending upon the endowments of the areas in which university is located. Vinoba has confidently argued that it is possible to offer the facilities for the highest education and research in the village to village universities. The earlier efforts to promote integrative education through organizations like "Vishwa Bharati" (set-up by Tagore) and "Aanter Bharti (set-up by Sane Guruji) should be revived and strengthened.

(10) Ideal Ashrami Education: Gandhi-Vinoba's Rules and Tenets (Shikshaka Ashrami Adarsha)

In his book, *India of My Dreams*, we find Gandhiji's beliefs, tenets (Manyataye) regarding education. They are reproduced below:

- Boys and girls, till they are eight years old, should be given the same education.
- Their time should be spent mainly in physical work; this should happen under the supervision of teachers. The physical work should be regarded as part of education.

- After ascertaining the taste of every girl and boy, he or she should be given the work.
- While taking any work, its cause should be known.
- Is man only an economic man (naked ape) or with a potential to become an angel?
- Satyagrah is one way to eliminate injustice and oppression.
- Education must be free from the State control.
- The medium of education should be mother tongue.
- The other languages can also be taught, but their place should not be compulsory or obligatory.
- The spiritual education should have a major place in it.
- The work or udyoga should also have a place in it.
- Teachers should be vanprasthashrami?
- The serious and honest efforts should be made for the reestablishment or reinstallation of a real teacher or an Acharya who should be impartial, fearless, enmityless, and vanprasthi.
- Let there be an "Acharyakul" of teachers as qualify now.
- When the boy or girl begins to understand, they should be given common knowledge. Their common knowledge should begin before they get the knowledge of alphabet.
- The alphabet (Akshar or varnamala) should be regarded a part of beautiful art of writing. The children should be taught to draw geometric figures, and when they get control over their fingers, they should be taught alphabet. It means that children should be taught to write beautiful handwriting from the beginning itself.
- Child should learn to read before he learns to write.
- Nothing should be taught to students by force or compulsion.
- Whatever children learn, they should learn in which they would get interest.
- Children's education should be like a play of any game. Play also is a part of education.
- Religious teaching should be a part of education, but it must be imparted through the behaviour, practice, etc.
- In the second 'Kala' or period also, boys and girls would be receiving education with boys, this would be a better arrangement.
- In the second period Hindu children should learn Sanskrit,

and Muslim children should learn Urdu or Arabic.

- In the second period, if it is possible to locate the work, vocation, profession with certainty, he should be taught in such a way that he chooses to adopt his father's work out of interest, and earn a living through it. This rule is not applicable to girls.
- The boys and girls should learn subjects like Maths, Geography, Botany, etc. by the age of 16 years. But they should also know stitching, preparing food, etc. The third period is 16 to 25 years.
- The education which begins after the nine years must be self-sufficient and self-reliant.
- The teachers should not get huge salaries. The schools do not need costly buildings.
- One should learn English as a language. English should be used for external trade and commerce.

These rules or tenets of ideal school can provide a rich food for thought to eliminate the drawbacks of the current sick educational institutions, and they can help to design a model system of education. Let us try to understand further Gandhiji's vision of a good education with the help of advice, criticism, suggestions aired by him from time to time.

(11) Nai Talim

The philosophy of Nai Talim should be widely spread among the public. This system of education would help to create and function the one-hour schools, family schools, and the ideal village Vidyapith. Chapter Seven in this book contains comprehensive discussion on Nai Talim.

As said earlier, Nai Talim synthesizes knowledge (dnan), action (Karma), and Ananda (bliss); it integrates shruti, smriti, and kriti, it would also integrates Yoga, Udyoga, and Sahayoga; it integrates place of work and parishramalaya and Vidyalaya. Its essence is "life through life". Nai Talim is a Swadeshi spirit, it drastically reduces the village-urban dichotomy. It would automatically solve current problems in education such as child labour, absenteeism, lack of black boards, classrooms, too many holidays, high drop-out rate, etc.

In Nai Talim, the teacher would be gramasevaka and not village servant; what he would earn would not be salary, it would be

"Dakshina". It would bring about a total Revolution or total socio-economic-political reconstruction; it would create a New-Man and New Society; it would be free from the State control, it would help to establish an Arcadian civilization with "Swaraj" or "Gramaswaraj".

Gandhi-Vinoba had developed the thought of Nai Talim very clearly and cleverly; they had emphasized that the "world of knowledge" and "World of Karma" are closely interrelated. They were not talking of professional education, employment, etc., they were talking of India's production system, agriculture etc., and how skills would be developed, and use them for gaining knowledge. But such a revolutionary thought was systematically rejected by India (which was a Himalayan Blunder). Kothari Commission was responsible for the death of Indian education. There is hardly much difference in education in India during the pre-independence and post-independence periods. Kothari Commission did not value Nai Talim more than "Work-experience".

As a part of educational reforms, education must be wedded to practical life: it should spring from ordinary experiences. It should encourage students to turn themselves (self-study); it should foster curiosity; what we need is the system of Individual Education.

The concept of BE is more relevant today than any time in the history of mankind.

Vinoba used to remind us that we should think of "Nitya Nai Talim and not just "Nai Talim". With the birth and growth of Bhoodana, "Gramadana", the scope, responsibility of people have increased. Beginning with "Bhoodana", we have taken the responsibility to bring about vast and deep work of non-violent revolution. This task cannot be completed without Nai Talim. Similarly, the work of Nai Talim cannot sustain "without success in Bhoodan-Gramadan. The gift of philosophy of *sarvodaya* can be spread throughout India with the help of Nai Talim.

(12) Deschooling or Nai Talim?

It was said that the state of education in the world including India is facing the crisis of survival. The best minds in the world are worried over the pathological state of education. We have presented a lot of empirical evidence in India and abroad to support the validity of such a view. The educational systems suffers from many and various ills, and it is harming instead of doing good to the society. Men like Gandhi-Vinoba have condemned the system in the strongest terms usually not found in their talks and writings.

What additional steps should we take so that education becomes and remains the greatest, vital resource? One suggestion is that all the schools should be closed or there should be deschooling of education? The other view is that the revolutionary transformation in the educational system through enlightened policies should be brought about. The second approach is a superior approach. The first approach would result in throwing the baby with bathwater.

(13) Self Reliance is an Essential Virtue

If the education in India is to become compulsory and easy, it is required that our educational institutions should become self-reliant. Similarly, our education can never be ideal if we regard international institutions such as World Bank, International Monetary Fund are accepted as role models. The purpose, goals, of IMF and World Bank are very superficial. They believe in the philosophy of globalization, marketization, etc. which have proved to have failed.

There has not been a dearth of literature on how to reform our educational system. There have been continuous debates about various aspects of education. Notwithstanding these, education has not progressed in the desired directions. The education has slided down from high to low. This has happened because non-issues have been posed as serious issues, the perception of the problems has been distorted. The approach to reforms has been conventional and not radical. The suggestions which have been made have been inadequate at their best, and harmful at their worst. Let us study them carefully.

(i) We have resorted to the arithmetic jugglery such as 11+4, 10+2+3, and back to 11+4 to improve the quality of education.

(ii) It has been argued that the classes should be small; teacher-students ratio should be high if education is to be quality education.

(iii) It has also been suggested that the matters would improve if the education is less specialization-oriented.

(iv) It is said that the problem we are facing is one of the conflict between quality on the one hand and the quantity or mass education on the other. At the higher level, the education should be for the few and not for the masses.

(v) We should adopt certain methods such as case study method, and we should make use of educational technology (transparencies, slides, video, etc.) for improving the quality of education.

(vi) The quality of education will improve if there is a greater interaction between industry and educational institutions.

(vii) It has also been argued that there should be greater intermingling of teaching and research for improving the quality.

(viii) For excellence in education, the engineers, technologists, doctors must learn about the effects of technology with the help of humanities and social science subjects; and liberal education students must learn about science and technology.

(ix) It has been suggested that: (a) early childhood education should be imparted in a professional way where "play way method" should be the watchword; (b) the ideal age for the entry into nursery school is 3.5 years and not earlier; (c) the admission tests for nursery schools should be abolished; (d) toy manufacturers and publishers should develop toys and materials which are child-friendly and which have educational value.

(x) In keeping with the ascendency of liberalization, it is now argued that education cannot improve unless it is privatized. Earlier, the argument was that it should be in the hands of the State. The good education is not a matter of ownership or control.

(xi) The often-used terms such as excellence and world quality in education also need to be redefined. All the conventional suggestions may not be useless, but they do not touch the roots of the problems; they reflect the preoccupation with the branches. As a result, there may be some reforms but certainly not the revolution.

(xii) The age of children should not be less than six years at the time of admission to school.

(xiii) The heavy burden of books should be reduced.

(xiv) The salaries of the teachers should be enough to eliminate all financial worries.

(xv) Fees should be minimum, and the State revenue should be used, government money should be spent more on primary education than on higher locations.

(xvi) The compulsory education should be done away with.

(xvii) Self-reliance and good manners should become the compulsory part of education.

(xviii) Education is not really getting degrees, it is a matter of total life philosophy.

(xix) Education must not be "*Sartha*"; it should be "*Samartha*", and "*Samagra*".

The physical or intellectual excellence is not enough. The IIT, for example, produces intellectually excellent students. But many of them are physically very weak. This means that we are not able to maintain even the physical health of our students. Excellence should encompass higher values—ethical, moral, character, etc. The excellence in education can come only if one understands the meaning of knowledge correctly. Education is for knowledge, and knowledge by definition, means the knowledge of the self, the knowledge of the relationship of the self with the body, the mind, the other beings, the nature, and the God. It is because of this meaning of knowledge that we say:

(a) "*Dnanam paramam dheyam*",

(b) "*Na hi Dnanem Sadhnishen paritramiha vidyate.*"

The level of excellence achieved by education will be proportional to the extent to which it serves to impart knowledge in this sense. The educational system which promotes ego, self-indulgence, self-interest, materialism, avarice greed would be far from excellence, howsoever costly, well-equipped, intellectually demanding, skills-promoting it happened to be.

(14) Three Levels of Values

One of the necessities to move education in appropriate direction is what emphasis is given on rural education. Gandhiji has said that his experiments have shown that education must reinforce the self-reliant rural life and in which suitable industry plays a crucial role in determining rural development.

(a) The lower level is more concerned about salaries, holidays, competition, profits-seeking, power.
(b) Middle level values are intellectual, logic skills, good citizenship.
(c) The highest value system comprises communitarian concerns, co-operation, self-control, honesty, etc.

(15) New Education for Rebuilding Moral India

Education must come through ordinary business of life. The teaching methods for the adult and child would generally be different. Audio method is suitable for adults, while stories, prayers, lives of saints are good for children. Children should not have to go through long-hours of teaching. Learning with the rest, and learning with excursion, learning by doing, learning by going nearer to the nature and society. Some important aspect of learning which cannot be taught orally should be taught through direct contact and experiencing learning through "eye on" and "hand on" experience.

New system of education would reconsider conceptualizations of teaching, learning and researching. Education encompassing a concern; or human rights; a culture of peace. Education is a fundamental element in all processes that aim to build a culture of peace, human rights. This involves something more than the provisions of information; it is a lifelong value-based process of improving knowledge and action within the framework of principles of truth, non-violence, satyagraha. In the context of deep human crisis in the 21st century, the education of future citizens heads to be redressed between academics and human rights.

The single minded focus on economic growth and globalization over much of 20th and 21st century has led to an erosion of human values. The making of moral citizens must mean persons with human excellence. The making of moral citizens must mean person with human excellence which includes strength of character, inner resources, family society and so on.

Connected to the question of excellence is the issue of ranking of Indian universities in relation to universities in various countries. Certain organizations in the world have come up with the statistics that not even one Indian university is in the list of top

200 which are assessed to be excellent and sought after by the foreigners. It is felt by many that this is a matter of worry for India. It may be noted that certain other assessments have argued that Indian education is far superior to education in other countries.

These issues cannot be tackled merely by changing educational formula such as 2+3+5. While planning for the educational system in the future, the wise policy would be to shun global competition. The Swadeshi and Swaraj are the best concepts over which a world-class educational system can be built.

The best minds in the world, viz. Russel, Hayek, Gandhi, Vinoba, Vivekananda have been perturbed or worried in the 20th Century. The vast numbers of people have been suffering from despair, loneliness, bewilderment, cynicism, and so on. This has been so in spite of ample, advanced know how.

Education plays a very important part in the birth, growth, and death of civilizations. Such is the importance of education in human life. Present human civilization is in crisis because today's education is in crisis. But the educational crisis cannot be tackled, the problems of education cannot be solved by mere organization, administration, or money. The education is breaking down not so much because of, say, over-specification but because of the absence of metaphysical awareness. We are suffering from a metaphysical disease, and the cure, therefore, must be metaphysical. Education which fails to clarify our central concerns is mere training or indulgence. For it is our central convictions that are in disorder, and, and as long as the present anti-metaphysical temper persists, the disorder will grow worse. Education, far from ranking as men's greatest resource, will then be an agent of destruction (Schumacher, 1965, pp. 70-92).

A. Huxley has argued that there are three main categories of defects—sacrifice of the individual to the system, psychologically unsound methods of teaching, and irrational methods of imposing discipline. We need a new system of universal education of the same kind as that which has proved itself. We need a system of individual education (*Selected Essays*, 1972, p. 60).

Gandhi-Vinoba have contributed a new galaxy of altogether original ideas, terms, concepts, programmes, viz. swadeshi, swaraj, Nai Talim, Satyagraha, and Constructive works programme (CWP). This programme is intimately connected with the revolution of education. It was meant to promote both basic education and the adult education. The primary aim of CWP was the elimination of illiteracy in India. In order to achieve this, Gandhi-Vinoba advocated that women also should be provided liberal education. And in order to ensure that this should happen actually, he recommended that women should be provided scholarships. CWP occupies unique importance in Gandhiana, i.e., Gandhian evolutionary and revolutionary mass-oriented, practical, wellbeing enhancing programming and other activities. His thinking on these programmes has influenced his philosophy of education.

Gandhiji restructured the curriculum such that manual labour and literary studies in a balanced manner which will release immense creative energies. The teaching of handicrafts as the pivot or centre of the whole educational programme would cultivate creative instincts. Such an educational system would involve reforms/revolution. The ultimate purpose of education would then be progress in rural areas or villages. "My plan is also to impart primary education through the medium of village handicrafts is thus conceived as the spearhead of silent social revolution fraught with the most far-reaching consequences. It will provide a healthy and moral basis of relationship between the city and village." (Glyn, p. 30)

(16) Miscellaneous Pre-requisites

Moolodyoga should be the basis of education. The Kothari Commission (appointed by the Government of India) used the word "work experience", which was a wrong thing to do. The word work experience does not convey the meaning and philosophy of moolodyoga. Vinoba has said the task of providing adult and primary education cannot be completed unless people resort to agitation. Unless the rulers and others show courage, the educational reforms cannot be carried out. Job and degree should be separated. The independence, autonomy of the universities must be protected at any cost. At present, there are many controls, restraints on educational institutions, they should be eliminated. Atomic, spiritual restrains should be replaced, and teachers (movement) should be started. Just as Bhoodan, Gramdan movements were started, teachers' movement should also be started. The teachers should take study tours, accumulate experiences and inform their views to the government. This will result in creating control or restraint on the rulers through the teachers.

(17) The Aandolan or Movement by teachers, and *Sarvodaya* workers would strengthen each other, and these two types of Aandolan would result in the increase in power, strength, authority of the teachers. This will result in the revival of villages which would lead to the revival of the republic. This will be the beginning of New Society culminating in due course into a new social system, social organization. It would provide guidance, advice, help to both Bharat and the world. We would then say with due pride, "Jai Jagat". India has made much progress in making Indian education "Saffron coloured", "Samyavadikaran", and "Rashtriyakaran". But one important thing that remains to be done is "Bhartiyakaran of education".

(18) Gandhi-Vinoba were very much dissatisfied, disillusioned with the then present educational system. Therefore, even at the cost of being misunderstood, both of them have asked the students to leave, desert their classrooms, their educational institutions. They used to say that it is the demand of this age that today's educational system should be buried deep at the earliest. It does not deserve to be buried with honour. Today's educational system is a bad thing, it is eating away our heart.

"Gramswaraj", "Panchayat", "Panch Parmeshwar" etc. is Bhartiya thought. Such social organization does not exist in other countries. "*Advait*, service, devotion, and productive work are the soul of this *Sanskriti*. The best part of Bhartiya Sanskriti is in the word "*Mahila*". There is no other word in any language in the world which is equal to that word. Mahila means great (Mahan) person or woman. The main place of *Bhartiya Sanskriti* is mother power or "*Matrushakti*".

We have to keep our rural civilization safe because the rural civilization is the only valuable civilization. The message of our civilization is that "dharma" and "Artha" walk together; they should work together.

(19) The curricular books being used today are harmful, and useless. The students should not need textbooks. It is the duty of teachers to get textbooks, study them and then impart quality education to students.

(20) To avoid spiritual bankruptcy, we have to leave space for religious education. The teachers must ask students to study all religions, and train them to be tolerant and acceptors of all religious truths.

(21) Adult education has a place in India's policy for education. The widespread illiteracy is a social strain. Illiteracy must, therefore, be reduced to the maximum. At the same time, it should be remembered that adult education does not mean knowledge of only alphabet.

(22) Gandhiji was not against higher education. But if priorities are to be set, he would want the nation to give higher priority or precedence to the primary education. After doing that if resources were available, then some help could be extended for the higher education. He was all for higher education if it was self-reliant.

(23) The educational system, if it is to be healthy must be founded on some real sector. In the Indian case, the education must be based on agriculture. Instead, the level and structure of agriculture have become distorted. All this will have to be reversed. The members will have to change their outlook in this connection. The (agri) culture has become (agri) business or (agri) commerce, or (agri) industry. This does not augur well for the Indian educational system.

(24) Which powers, authority of the universities should remain with the State, and which ones should be available to the teachers, should be decided after due deliberations. It stands to reason that Centre, States, will not have much powers to interfere in the functioning of vidyapiths. In each village, one subject should be studied, and in the case of small villages, their surroundings should be unified and attached with one of the Vidyapiths. There should be decentralization of facilities for studying various subjects in all places. Today, the teacher, the Acharya is like a bullock who merely carries out the decisions taken by the governments. This picture must change. As stated elsewhere also, he should possess three qualities, he should guide, counsel, advise students, he should love his students, he should be studious, and he should shun politics.

In other words, the aim of educational revolution is to bring about the confluence of "dnan" and "karma", the renunciation of egoism and "Vasanas", non-violent change, and compassionate education.

(25) It is imperative that the medium of instruction and education must be the mother tongue. The educational revolution requires that a correct language philosophy is implemented. This, in turn, depends on giving mother tongue and Sanskrit their legitimate place. Vinoba has conveyed the importance of Sanskrit by mentioning its characteristics, merits. According to him, Sanskrit is a language of spirituality. It contains spiritual *Vidya* and Brahmavidya; Sanskrit is a language of spreading Sanskriti. She is a mother of all languages. Sanskrit is a living language. Sanskrit is a language of "Manava dharma". Sanskrit united India. Gandhiji and Vivekananda also believed in this.

(26) Gandhi-Vinoba have been a staunch, unswerving supporter of the idea that mother tongue should be the medium of education. In spite of some support to the idea favouring mother tongue, English has become a medium of education in India. This is unfortunate. It is our thoughtless attachment (Moha) which is making us favour English as a medium. Both were perceptive enough to foresee the consequences of the use of foreign language, which touched upon inter-community harmony, etc. They had told that when we get education through our mother tongue, our relationship with other members of house becomes strong; we would make our wives real life-companion, we would be able to establish relationship with mother, father, dhobi, nai, today. The way in which we are insulting our mother tongues, we will have to do penance for this sin. The common man has suffered quite a great deal due to our language policy. Our belief in the knowledge of English has made us slaves. They told us that this belief has made us incapable of rendering true service.

It is imperative that the coming years should halt, stop, policy such as our national policy, language policy, mother tongue policy, or cradle has made available.

(27) Perhaps everywhere, but definitely so in India, mother plays a great role in educating children. In Marathi, there is a proverb which says, "Jichya hati Palnyachi dori ti jagate udhari" (it means the person who holds the rope of the cradle, uplifts the world). The mother is the best teacher in the world. This role should be further enhanced such that we should be able to say, "Matru mukhan Shikshanam" and "Matru hasten bhojanam". It means, we get educated through the mother's mouth, and we get food from the hands of mother, thus, the mother, father, family, gurukul are the centres of education. The education must be provided through mother-teacher. The important pre-requisites for educational transformation are listed below:

- Revive Bhartiya Sanskriti (Indian Culture), Indian philosophy, and unity so on.
- Rethink and Revive Varnashram Dharm or varnashram system.
- We must revive the "Gurukul" system of education. Revive the relationship of Gurumawooli. Acceptance and recognition of spirituality and healthy religiosity and rejection of materialism.
- Vrat chintan, vrat practice as far as possible.
- The 12 *vratas* to guide individual and societal entities. The inspiration for leading a healthy life to be drawn from "Bhartiya Sanskriti".
- Revival of Sanyas Ashram; Revival of practice of *"Yati Dharma"* and *"Parivrajak tradition"*.
- Change of man, making a new man, change of heart, mind through genuine education to be imparted. Thus "Lok shikshan" on a wide scale for transformation. Gandhi-Vinoba insisted that vrataha, spirituality for every body and not only for "sadhakaha"; they are not only for individuals that also for community. All of these are not only for Sadhak, but for Sansarics also.
- The revival of Sanskrit language and study of Sanskrit literature.
- Hindi to be made "Rashtra Bhasha".
- Revival of ideal Guru-shishya tradition.
- To establish "Acharyakul"
- Decentralization of nearly everything
- Practice of "Sarvadharma" collective prayers
- *Vimukta shiksha*—Nai Talim for any kind of education
- Vinoba has said with emphasis that it is imperative that Bhartiya *"Shikshan Shastra"* (science of education) should be definitely revived. It should be kept in mind that *"Bhartiya Shikshan Shastra"* is based on the thought of Shri Krishna.
- Similarly, everybody should make efforts to revive and make active Indian ethos.

- All the people must become worshipers of freedom and knowledge
- Education must be promotive of non-violence
- Education must be independent of the State and the rich. Police will not be allowed to enter campuses.
- Vinoba pointed out that the whole country is like a campus, and, therefore, there is no need, no place for the police in the country.
- Vinobaji has also said that the school is not a place for teaching, it is a centre of development of the child. The development of individual personality should occur on the basis of basic education. The parental education would lead to "Vyakti vikas" (Individual development). In short, chirantan education; Vyakti vikas, experience-based education, development of basic education, free, self-governing education, and free, compulsory education are prerequisites of educational revolution.

Deschooling as Nai Talim

Some educational systems debated in the world are: (1) Home schooling, (2) Unschooling, (3) Resisting schooling, (4) Deschooling society, (5) Free domestic schooling, (6) Vimukta shiksha, (7) Nai Talim. It is not our intention to discuss here all these "alternatives". The systems like Unschooling, Resisting schooling, home schooling reflect the phenomenon of terminological development; they did not encompass all the major issues, they are not widely known and discussed widely, and they are relatively new addition to the literature on our topic. Some scholars are now talking about deschooling the Humanity.

The Vimukta Shiksha celebrates the courage and wisdom of those individuals, families and communities who are trying to resist being schooled/conditioned/ institutionalized/dehumanized and, in the process are trying to reclaim control of their own-learning/lives.

What is a School?

The schools are institutions which require full-time attendance. It is the age-specific, teacher-related process requiring full-time attendance for obligatory curriculum. It is built on the axiom that learning is the result of teaching. The schools tend to make a total claim on the time and energy of the participants. This, in turn, makes the teacher into custodian, preacher, therapist. The teacher as the custodian acts as a master of ceremonies. The teacher as a moralist is a substitute for parents, even God. He decides what is good and what is bad for the pupil.

Why deschooling or disestablishment? According to Illich, many students, teachers, and others intuitively know what the schools do for them. The institutionalization of values leads inevitably to physical pollution, social polarization, and psychological impotence, the process of degradation.

What does schooling of society mean? Not only education but social reality itself has become schooled. It costs roughly the same to school both rich and poor. The yearly expenditure for pupil in the slums and in the rich suburbs lies in the same range everywhere, not only education but society as a whole needs deschooling.

The intellectuals, like Ivan Illich (II), are convinced that the universal education through schooling is not feasible even if attempts were made to do so. Ivan Illich has developed his philosophy of deschooling on the basis of certain beliefs. They are:

(1) The right to learn is curtailed by the obligation to go to schools.
(2) The ethos, not just the institutions of society ought to be deschooled.
(3) All over the world, the school has an anti-education effect on society.
(4) Escalation of the school is as destructive as the escalation of the weapons but less visibly so.
(5) The illusion on which school is founded is that learning happens casually and as by-product of some other activity.

Neither the new attitudes of teachers nor the proliferation of educational hardware or software can deliver universal education. Illich has, therefore, suggested the idea of deschooling. What is deschooling?

All the world over, the education is very costly, very complex, impossible task to perform. The schools appropriate money, men, good-will, and other resources available for education. The present schooling, its addition, discourages other institutions from allowing them to perform. The obligatory schooling inevitably polarizes the society.

There are certain changes which will occur in education in a deschooled society:

(a) The schools would be replaced by "learning networks", or "learning webs", or "communication webs".
(b) In this system, there will be self-motivated learning. Knowledge would be a function of an active engagement in real-life situations.
(c) The control of persons and institutions in educational values would be abolished.
(d) The sharing of skills would be liberated.
(e) The critical and creative resources of the people would be liberated.
(f) Individuals would be provided with opportunities or freedom to entrust himself to the teacher, guide, adviser, healer of his choice.
(g) The teacher would provide help in achieving learning tasks initiated by the learner himself.
(h) Education should be open to every person and it would be through life.
(i) Ivan Illich used to think that traditional village system of education was very good. But he felt that it is not practical to return to it.

The educational paradigms namely, Nai Talim conceived by Gandhiji, and the Deschooling conceived by Ivan Illich in 1937 and 1971 are similar to each other. But they are not same. The idea of Nai Talim preceded the idea of Deschooling at least by 35 years. As Illich himself appears to have once acknowledged that what he and other Western scholars were thinking in 1950s, Gandhi-Vinoba had thought about long back. It has not been implemented so far.

The people in the West as well as in the East have deserted the wisdom of the wise. They have not shown the courage, the conviction, sagacity to put in practice the vision of Gandhiji, Vinoba, and Ivan Illich.

Appendix

Thoughts-Grains
(*Vichar Kanika* or *Vichar Kana*)

India has a strong, widely used tradition of formulating and using "Sutras" to convey the meaning in discourse. To recall, Sutras are short, pithy, statements which contain great wisdom. The Sages like Vinoba and Gandhi have a writing style which consists of statements which are similar to Sutras. The search or gleaning of literature has yielded a number of such statements some of which have been presented here.

Before proceeding, let it be pointed out that such wise statements are differently called by different people. For example, wise thoughts grains, Vichar Kanika, Vichar-Kana, Vachane, Vichar, Vichar particles, Vichar grains, Suvarna grains, Golden grains, and Honey drops. They have been collected from Vinoba, Vichar pothi; Vinoba, Vinoba Sahitya, Gandhi's sources. They would be deemed to be convenient and useful for general use, although they are intended to aid particularly those who are studying the philosophy of education.]

1) Spiritual activity means natural activity or pure activity.
2) The best service is the service of guests, sants, miserable, and those who hate us.
3) Untruth has no strength or power; it has to take shelter of truth even for its existence.
4) Truth, restraint, and service constitute the trimurti of spiritual life.
5) The seed of death is the desire to live. If that desire vanishes, death is dead.
6) To love enemy is safe.
7) I do not like to be high like a mountain. If my "mitti" is cast or spread on me, I would be happy.
8) Sadhak should be alert even in sleep. It is necessary for exploration of the self.
9) Nai Talim is a life philosophy.
10) "*Sarvodaya* Patra" offer women a means to do some small and easy works. When this idea occurred to Vinoba, he said that he had become a Rishi.
11) Women must practise self-control or self-restraint. If the woman becomes self-controlled, she will have control over society.
12) Males have given women not only gold but also attachment to gold.

13) There is love among women and men, but if there is no detachment and knowledge along with love, the freedom will elude us.
14) Nature-cure is not founded on a lot of knowledge; it is founded on devotion to God. Nature cure treatment has been called "Satva" diagnosis.
15) Complete sleep, suitable body labour, sky intake, limited eating are the four nature treatments.
16) As the science progresses, means of enjoyment (indulgence) will increase, yearning (craving) for enjoyment will decline.
17) In the age of science desire to enjoy will be minimum, but means of enjoyment will be plenty.
18) So far we have experienced three states (conditions, situations):
    (a) Country dependent or under foreign rule—villages under self-rule;
    (b) Both nation and villages under foreign rule;
    (c) Country free but villages under alien rule.
    We have now to work for making both country and villages free, independent.
19) "Let us go to villages" was and still is a "Mantra" which, if it is understood well, India would be uplifted.
20) (i) Today's knowledge, learning, know-how (vidya) have become the servant of money and power.
    (ii) All teachers have become servants.
    (iii) Guru-disciple relationship has vanished.
    (iv) The brains of students are being subjected to regimentation.
21) Now the whole education (vidya) is only in the schools, colleges, and universities. The one who can pay the fees can partake in it. The meaning of higher education is that *vidya* which enables us to loot our brothers.
22) (i) Teachers should walk for some time in a pure and open air. They should walk for at least 4 to 5 miles daily in the open air.
    (ii) Teachers should go to bed early. They should go to sleep by maximum 8.00 o'clock. Let there be pitch dark when they sleep. They should go to sleep in silence. Teachers ought to sweat daily.
23) Instead of calling Gandhiji's birth-day or death-day as either "Gandhi Jayanti" or "Charkha Jayanti". We should call it as "*Sarvodaya* day".
24) Gandhiji's workers can be called "Khadi Parivar", "*Sarvodaya* Parivar" or "Gandhi Parivar". Gandhi parivar is Rishi's name, "*Sarvodaya* Parivar" is Mantra's name, and "Khadi Parivar" is Tantra's name.
25) One should not be scared without any cause. God's name may be chanted if one is afraid of something.

26) The mistakes we commit should be corrected on the same day.
27) Understand any thought fully and determine strongly to implement it.
28) If there is a need, help others. Never forget that you have received help frequently from others.
29) Do not take a meal unless and until you do some physical labour that is productive.
30) Study daily regularly for some time.
31) Always speak the truth. Always behave truthfully.
32) Never get angry; anger is a symptom of weakness.
33) Do not always serve your self-interest. Always keep in mind that this world is not for your enjoyment, we exist to serve this world.
34) Do not see others' defects or shortcomings, see their good qualities only.
35) Be unhappy or sorrowful by seeing others' sorrow, and make all efforts to reduce others' sorrow.
36) Be satisfied with a little. Do not be rude. Be soft-spoken.
37) Do not cross the limits. Be ashamed of doing bad things. Avoid unnecessary movements of your body and its parts.
38) Do not give in if somebody wishes you to be suppressed by his physical strength.
39) If some weak person commits an error, forgive him.
40) If there is a body-pain, have patience and courage.
41) Pay attention to the cleanliness.
42) Do not be jealous of any one. Do not put someone down in order to lift up yourself.
43) If man's speech becomes pure, he becomes speech-realized (*vacha siddha*).
44) My work needs neither publicity, nor psychological perfection, nor psychic power; it needs purity.
45) There should be humility in speech. One wants steadfastness, and broadness of intellect; we should keep on doing our work. The work will be completed by His grace, but we will be instruments in His hands.
46) Today's "Sadhana" consists of Rama in heart, name of God, and service of the public.
47) Only when the body is rubbed in service, we receive "aatmadnyan".
48) All people have good and bad qualities. Bad qualities are those of "Maya", and good qualities are those of God.
49) The own satisfaction is the true wealth. We obtain "Aatma Sukha" that is the final virtue.
50) Instead of widening the scope of Karma, we should increase its depth.

51) When the man does not discard work or efforts (but) when he leaves out I-ness, his prayer does not fail.
52) We are here for two days. We have to give maximum love, sacrifice, and service.
53) Opponents should be used for purifying our "chitta".
54) It is very necessary to practise at least one-hour speechless time. This practice helps the individual to make his life ever fresh.
55) From spiritual point of view, everyone must have some agricultural (cultivable) land.
56) The more the man soars up, the less the people understand and know him.
57) Jai Hari in heart, Jai Jagat in speech, and Jai Hind in practice will save us all.
58) Due to delusion, false attachment, we do our householder's work with devotion. Similarly, we should do society's work with great love, devotion, interest.
59) Apart from Bhoodan, Gramadana, there are other "danas" like "Abhayudan", and "fast-dan". The person who has detached himself from the body alone can give "Abhayudan".
60) What is "Pap" and "Punya"? Whatever gives us mental peace is "Punya", and the thing takes away the peace is "Pap".
61) Music and drawing are fine arts. But cooking is a finer art.
62) Everybody has his strength, and also the limitations. We should encourage the growth of each other's strength, and repair the limitations.
63) There are many fathers and mothers in the world whose children direct the world affairs. But those fathers and mothers whose children guide "Paramarth" deserve kudos.
64) Gita is the definition of "Ramanama". The simplicity of life reflects the "Ramanama".
65) There is little benefit in repaying enmity by enmity. There is little special in repaying goodness by goodness. To repay enmity by goodness alone is the correct path.
66) All have a right on me, but I have right on no one. If we fathom this, we would be always happy.
67) The praise is more dangerous than criticism, the praise is like a sweet poison.
68) Faith is a basic value or quality.
69) Vedic Rishis were the seers of "Mantras", not their creator. Therefore, the meaning of Mantra keeps on growing day by day.
70) Newspaper is one which contains no news.
71) Dhritrashtra was blind. The spiritual meaning of blindness is false attachment (Moha). If our mind is full of Moha or attachment, we should regard such people also as blind.
72) If we want to rest the body and mind, the best means are sound sleep and remembering God's name (Namasmaranam).

73) Grihasthashram = Truth and Self-control + Liking for service.
74) More production is the only way to fight inflation. Lack of finance is our strength, not our weakness.
75) Truth alone matters in satyagraha, not aagraha. Satyagraha means our own non-insistence.
76) We should live everywhere without insistence. When we become Agraha-Mukta, Vigraha-Mukta, Sangraha-Mukta, and "grahamukta", this planet will become a divya-bhavya Swarga.
77) *Sarvodaya* is "Ramanama" for us.
78) Bhoodan does not involve only Parameshwar. The goal of Bhoodan is not only obtaining some land, the goal is to join the hearts together.
79) Only that country whose citizens have obtained control, restraint, over their mind can be free.
80) Vedant-based Ahimsa can help us to establish Mangal everywhere. We would like to bring about integration in values. We want to break Mamta (attachment), and equality is to be promoted. Rama's faith is Truth, Krishna's detachment, Buddha's compassion are our heritage.
81) We should not be in an illusion, delusion that our work will bring about some big changes in life.
82) There should be three things in Ashramas: (a) discussion on knowledge and science; (b) discussion on life-research; (c) service to the surroundings.
83) If there is insistence along with thought, mark that it means that the thought is bad.
84) There will be no need for the army in the nation which possesses good teachers and good education.
85) The thought alone is our weapon, our "Shastra", our "Shastra" do not possess any other strength than thought. Vichar Tantra, Mantra.
86) Individuals have heart, institutions, have constitution and rules; they have "tantra" and "Mantra". We do not possess any other strength than thought.
87) If the cow survives, rural areas will survive, the nation and her culture and civilization will survive.
88) Study Sanskrit. The study of Sanskrit is essential if Indian culture is to be protected.

[A few "Vichar-Kana" could be given below with the names of their authors.]

89) The aim of education is nothing less than shaping the individual, making a New Man, building nations, and saving the civilizations. Education helps the man to develop his intelligence and reasoning; it cultivates good habits in man; it effects behaviour modification in people. Education enables man to

realize higher values in life which are essential for making man the crowning glory of the creation. (Mahatma Gandhi [MG])

90) Education is the greatest and the most valuable resource. (E.F. Schumacher)

91) Today, the schools and colleges have turned out to be factories for producing clerks for the government. (Mahatma Gandhi)

92) Education should be so revolutionized as to answer the wants of the poorest villager instead of answering those of Imperial exploiter. (Mahatma Gandhi)

93) Education is the art of drawing out full manhood. Education should result in all-round drawing out of the best in child and man—in body, mind and spirit. (Mahatma Gandhi)

94) Literacy is not the end of education or even a beginning. (Mahatma Gandhi)

95) Education must be through life, for life, and throughout life. (Mahatma Gandhi)

96) To think of education as a means of earning livelihood or living or employment betrays an unworthy disposition and mind. (Mahatma Gandhi)

97) The education that does not teach us to discuss and to discriminate between good and bad is a fruitless education. (Mahatma Gandhi)

98) In school, registered students submit to certified teachers to obtain certificate of their own. Both are frustrated, and both blame "insufficient resources" and infrastructure for their mutual frustration. (Carnagie Commission)

99) The right to learn is curtailed in the obligations to attach and attend the school. (Ivan Illich)

100) All over the world, the school has an anti-education effect on society. (Ivan Illich)

101) The escalation of the school is as destructive as the escalation of weapons but less visibly so. (Ivan Illich)

102) Instead of equalizing chances, the school system has monopolized their distribution. (Ivan Illich)

103) My grandmother wanted me to have an education, so she kept me out of school. (Margaret Meade)

104) What did you learn in the school? I learnt that what you sign for and what you get are two different things. (Charles Schultz)

105) The first-hand knowledge is the ultimate basis of intellectual life. To a large extent, book-learning conveys second hand information and as such can never rise to the importance of immediate practice. What a learned world offers is second hand scrap of information. The second handedness of the learned world is the secret of mediocrity. (A.N. Whitehead)

106) Sa *Vidya* Ya Vimuktaye. (ancient wisdom)
107) No country can become a nation by producing a race of translators. (Mahatma Gandhi)
108) The supreme aim of education should be to change the attitudes of the children and ultimately of the whole people—the values of the people as a whole. (Myrdal)
109) Education is such a main key that by using it, we can open each and every department, aspect of life. (J.C. Kumarappa)
110) Mass public education was clearly a humanizing step forward ... next to life and liberty. We consider education the greatest blessing bestowed upon mankind. But what passes for education today, even in our best schools and colleges is a hopeless anachronism. (Alvin Toffler)
111) Religion is the manifestation of divinity of man and education is the manifestation of the perfection in man. (Mahatma Gandhi)
112) The Indian educational system is ten times better than the UK system.
113) It is no exaggeration to say that a human being without education is not far removed from an animal. I did not believe in the existing system of education. (Mahatma Gandhi)
114) The problematique of education cannot be solved unless it is entrusted to "mother-teacher" or "Teacher-mother". (Mahatma Gandhi)
115) English education would create a generation of brown "Sahibs", and interpreters between the millions whom we govern, a class of persons Indian in blood and colour but English in tastes, in opinions. (Macaulay)
116) Character building, character advancement, character preservation, making students courageous ought to be the aim of education. This is for more important than mere literacy or bookish education. (Mahatma Gandhi)
117) Among different levels of education, i.e., primary, secondary and university education, some people would like to give more importance to university education than say, primary education.
118) The goal of education must coincide with the larger life-purpose. All human beings ultimately desire to be happy. The aim of education is to provide this life-long happiness to human beings. (Mahatma Gandhi)
119) Plants are shaped by cultivation and men by education. (Rousseau)
120) Education consists in the cultivation of instincts and not to suppress them. (B. Russel)
121) Basic education links the children to all that is best and lasting in India. (Mahatma Gandhi)

122) We have taken away the life out of education; the cancer has so eaten into the society that, in many cases, the only meaning of education is the knowledge of English. (Mahatma Gandhi)

123) True education must correspond to the surrounding circumstances (Mahatma Gandhi)

124) I do regard spinning and weaving as a necessary part of any national system of education. (Mahatma Gandhi)

125) In the context of deep human crisis in the 21 century, the education of future citizens needs to be redressed in order to achieve a better balance.

126) The end of all education should surely be service, and if the student gets an opportunity of rendering service even when he is studying he should seize it. (Mahatma Gandhi)

127) The real difficulty is that people do not know how to evaluate education. We tend to assess education as we assess land, gold, shares etc. We hardly give any thought to the improvement of the character of the educated. The girls, we say, need not earn, and, therefore, they need not learn. As long as such an attitude prevails, there is no hope to arrive at or knowing the true value of education. (Mahatma Gandhi)

128) The best function of education is to enable us to realize that to live as man is great, and it requires profound philosophy for its ideal, poetry for its expression, and heroism in its conduct. (Tagore)

129) Education is that sequence of growth through which the individual slowly adjusts to social atmosphere, and also adopts ethical values. (Raman)

130) The aim of education is to help individual to grow. It wants man to become man, and to develop mutual communion.

131) We need education which can help us in creating character, increasing strength and subuddhi, and character, which results in increase in our strength. It leads to growth of subuddhi and it enables us to stand on our own legs. (Vivekananda)

132) Education without courage is like a wax-statue—beautiful to look at, but which is bound to melt at the first touch of hot stuff.

133) It is impossible to get from "outside" what does not exist "inside". We can get from this world externally only that and that much whose seeds are within us. In other words, if there is no water in the well, you will not get it in a water drawing vessel.

134) The interest or liking of education tends to vanish when the pupil comes to feel that he is getting an education or that he is being educated.

135) The artificial feeling that education is a duty is very much inferior to the natural feeling that education is a joy.

136) The education of the pupils should take place without one being aware of it like the child learns his mother tongue.
137) If the individual is fundamentally or basically or by nature evil, there is no hope for (his) education.
138) The regime of punishment rules where there is no hope for education.
139) The fundamental belief that "every man has a soul" is the basis of Satyagraha and education.
140) The thoughtful philosophers and educationists have put forth the scientific law that all the tenets of the Completeness or Absolute are self-proved or self-obtained, or self-realized in the form of seeds.
141) The goal of education is to make men better citizens.
142) Unless the Guru himself is a natural, true, native (sahaj) and exclusive (Ananya) teacher, the students will not get natural (sahaja) education.
143) We must get education through the act of living itself.
144) The education that is given (imparted) is no education at all. The method of giving education is no method at all.
145) Unless we exercise in continuous action, we do not get appetite for knowledge.
146) The natural consequence of knowledge is that then one does not get bored.
147) How to live without opposing, contesting any one is the best education which includes all education. (sarvashama avirodhen).
148) In education, we must first make provision for food, and then only think of imparting knowledge
149) Labour is our deity.
150) Children do not belong to their parents only; they belong to the society too.
151) In India, the large number of people that have knowledge-related manual are the result of abandoning physical labour.
152) If the children remain dependent on others after being educated, their education can be said to have gone.
153) Education does not take place only through our capacity to talk. The message is: Live your life and get the education in turn.
154) The whole of constructive works programme is a programme of love.
155) To achieve completeness or totality is the goal of life of man.
156) Only when educated city people and the villagers from your rural areas become one, the kranti will happens.
157) The Kranti in India will take place only when the leaders become one or united or integrated.
158) A teacher must be good management expert or manager.

159) If the mental advancement of Tukaram can occur in small village like Dehu, then why similar progress in Delhi is needed?
160) Humility or humbleness is the key for opening the treasure.
161) The teacher will not see anything or any action from the external perspective; he will do so from the internal perspective.
162) Mental development is what the education should try to achieve.
163) Only those who have performed something valuable, big, should be given right to teach.
164) The objective of education is not merely to create suitable persons for work; the aim is to bring about development of qualities of people. The goal is not merely to create skilled, educated, expert personnel; it is to bring about the total development of the man. Thus, development of qualities in man towards total or all-dimensional development of human beings ought to be the aim of education.
165) The intellect warmed up due to physical labour is ready and keen to absorb knowledge, it becomes fruitful or it bears fruits. We do not intend to thrust, press knowledge in pupils. We intend to make pupils strong enough to receive knowledge. Beyond this, the pupil learns on his own.
166) We need to have an ideal combination of knowledge and appropriate ignorance (lack of knowledge).
167) Initial or beginning education is not the only meaning of Buniyadi education. Whatever education we give to students must be based on value system.
168) Knowledge should not be unripe. The knowledge that is backed by deed or practice will never remain unripe.
169) The entry of "tantra" in the field of education is undesirable.
170) Nai Talim is a system of thought, it is not "Tantra". Nai Talim is a system of self-control.
171) The education of small children must be left in the hands of women.
172) We must always remember that we are separate from both the mind and body. To educate people about this philosophy is a true education. To know the self is the highest virtue.
173) The Basic Education scheme had visualized that till one reaches 16 years of age, there will be education of self-reliance; and after the age of 16, it would be self-dependent.
174) Rural University is one in which education would be for all parts.
175) We get knowledge through action (karma), karma gets completed through *vidya* or gyana, and two together results in chitta-vikas.
176) If India introduces Nai Talim, the high-low, rich-poor dichotomies would disappear. The labour would get its high

status. The society would get good sevaks and rakshak. Every village will be self-reliant.

177) In respect of education, it can be said that lengths and widths are not relevant in studying and educating.

178) In schools, there is no need for holidays. If we like, if we have joy in knowledge i.e. if men are glad, where is the need for holiday.

179) Only the teachers are strong enough to bring about bloodless, ahimsak, kranti.

180) Nai Talim means establishment of new values. When there will be greater, widespread attraction for new values, Nai Talim will spread.

181) There is a "Life-view" or "world view" at the back of Nai Talim. Nai Talim may fall, there may be failure of the scheme if societies are unable to develop attraction for new value system of Nai Talim. One dimensional or partial understanding of Nai Talim, and distorted imitation can lead to the failure of Nai Talim.

182) Shasan-Mukti is the self-realized right which cannot be tampered with.

183) Teacher, Minister, leader should get similar salary. What the teacher gets is "Dakshina" and not salary.

184) Nai Talim means one-hour schooling.

185) Shruti, Smriti, and Kriti stated in nutshell is the science of education.

186) Buniyadi education is a kind of sea. All different rivers of knowledge meet in that sea. The man-woman, city-village, and other such dualities vanish in Nai Talim.

187) Only the knowledge that is appropriate for the occasion or event should be given.

188) In the life and in education, Karma yoga is of great importance. The knowledge that cannot be given with work should be forgotten. Nai Talim would increase the income of the country.

189) The basic difference between Nai Talim and the current Talim is that history, maths, grammar, books, etc. are taught at present. In a new system it is life (and not individual subjects) would be taught.

190) So far I have not seen any Basic Educational School of my concept.

191) Basic education scheme came to be conceived in the Indian situation, it is a natural inspiration which gave birth to this idea. We should impart education from the surrounding or nearby nature.

192) Our every work is related with every other work, and all our works, are related to our life-style. Due to this life becomes joyful.

193) To learn while working is the vision of Nai Talim.
194) Today's Teacher is not a teacher, he is only a beast of burden.
195) The real education is the one that co-ordinates Head, Heart, and Hands, and puts to use all the five fingers.
196) Education is the manifestation of the perfection already in man.
197) Children should learn to read before they learn to write.
198) Nothing should be taught to students by force or compulsion.
199) Whatever children learn, they should learn in which they have interest.
200) Children's education should be like a play of any game. Play also is a part of education.
201) The children's education must take place in Mother tongue.
202) Religious teaching should be a part of education, but it must be imparted through their behaviour, practices, etc.
203) Hindu children should learn Sanskrit, and Muslim children should learn Urdu or Arabic.
204) If it is possible to locate the work, vocation, profession with certainty, he should be taught in such a way that he chooses to adopt his father's work out of interest, and earn a living through it. This rule is not applicable to girls.
205) The boys and girls should learn subjects like Maths, Geography, Botany, etc. by the age of 16 years. But they should also know stitching, preparing food, etc.
206) The education which begins after nine years must be self-sufficient and self-reliant.
207) The teachers should not get huge salaries. The schools do not need costly buildings.
208) One should learn English as a language. English should be used for external trade and commerce.

These rules or tenets of ideal school can provide a rich food for thought to eliminate the drawbacks of the current sick educational institutions, and they can help to design a model system of education. Let us try to understand further Gandhiji's vision of a good education with the help of advice, criticism, suggestion aired by him from time to time.

The philosophy of Nai Talim should be widely spread among the public. This system of education would help create and function the one-hour schools, family schools, and the ideal village vidyapith.

Glossary

1.	Acharya	: teacher
2.	Advait	: absence of duality
3.	Agni	: (god of) fire
4.	Ahimsa	: non-violence
5.	Ananda	: pleasure
6.	Anandi	: happy
7.	Anushasan	: discipline
8.	Ashrama-Shallas	: Ashrama-schools
9.	Avidya	: absence of knowledge, rites
10.	Bhoodan	: giving away one's own land willingly
11.	Brahmacharya	: abstinence
12.	Charaivati	: keep going
13.	Charkha	: a small machine for spinning cotton
14.	Dnan	: awareness
15.	Fakir	: who owns no wealth
16.	Gramdan	: entrusting their village's affairs (to the wishes of Vinoba Bhave)
17.	Hasta-sanyat	: control of hands
18.	Karuna	: compassion
19.	Langoti	: inner loin cloth
20.	Loksangraha	: hold on people
21.	Moksha	: emancipation
22.	Mukti	: emancipation
23.	Nai Talim	: New Education; Deschooling
24.	Nisarga	: nature
25.	Pad-sanyat	: control of feet
26.	Panchyam / Panchniyam	: five pledges
27.	Patanga	: moth
28.	Prem	: love
29.	Sadnan	: right knowledge
30.	Sahaj	: natural, easy
31.	Sakshatkar	: meeting/seeing in person
32.	Sarva Shiksha Abhiyan	: education for all

33. Sarvodaya : upliftment of all
34. Satya / Satyam : truth
35. Shanti : peace
36. Shlokas : hymns
37. Sukhi : happy/comfortable
38. Sukhi bhava : be happy
39. Sutra : formula
40. Swantah sukhaya : for one's own sake
41. Swaraj : self rule
42. Takli : a small hand-held tool for spinning cotton to make thread
43. Vacha-sanyat : control of speech
44. Vichar kana : droplets of thought
45. Vidnan : science
46. Vidya : knowledge, meditation
47. Vratas : pledges
48. Vyakti : person
49. Vyavaharic : practical
50. Samyayoga : the yoga of equality
51. Satyagraha : seeking truth, Gandhiji used it to mobilise people to oppose the British Empire
52. Gram Swaraj : autonomy to village
53. Samanvayacharya : an acharya who coordinates; an acharya who treats all equally
54. Drashta : one who sees
55. Bhashyakar : commentator
56. Shastri : a degree in Sanskrit, equal to BA
57. Krantdarshi : visionary of revolution
58. Sutrakar : one who composes or comments thoroughly and in detail
59. Antyodaya : upliftment of backward groups
60. Karmayoga : the yoga of action
61. Stitprandaya : one who has equanimity towards pleasure and pain
62. Grihasta ashram : the second section out of four envisaged by ancient seers, the state of married life
63. Satyayuga ki wapasy : return of the first Yuga in Hindu mythology
64. Sadhana : penance
65. Yajana : havan
66. Vanprasthashram : the third section out of four envisaged by ancient seers, the state of living in a secluded place

67. Sanyashashram : the fourth section out of four envisaged by ancient seers, the state of renunciation
68. Gurukul : Indian traditional schooling system
69. Gurugrih : the living quarters of the Guru
70. Rishiruna : debt owed to the teacher
71. Brahmanyak : commentaries on the Vedas
72. Aarvanyak : commentaries on the Vedas
73. Shabd vidya : science of letters
74. Shilpa vidya : sculptural science
75. Chikitsa vidya : medical science
76. Hetu vidhya : logic
77. Shravana : listening
78. Munis : thinkers
79. Rishis : seers
80. Àranyak : medical science
81. Shruti : the Vedas
82. Smriri : code of conduct
83. Kriti : a deed
84. Vidya sah yoga : education along with yoga
85. Buniyad : foundation
86. Sushikshata : good education
87. Moha : belonging
88. Panthas : faiths
89. Karam yoga : the yoga of action
90. Dnan yoga : the yoga of knowledge
91. Snatak : graduate
92. Sanghshakti : the strength of unity
93. Prakhanda : block

Select References

Aggarwal, J.C., and Gupta, S., *Great Philosophers and Thinkers on Education*, Shipra Publications, Delhi, 2006.

Allan Bloom, The closing of American Mind, 1987.

Allen Douglas, "Introduction: Key Issues and Overview of Gandhi's Philosophy for Twenty first Century" (Publication details unavailable).

Allen Douglas, "Mahatma Gandhi's Philosophy of Violence, Non-violence, and education" (Publication details unavailable).

Ananthu, T.S., *Going Beyond the Intellect: A Gandhian Approach to Scientific Education*, Gandhi Peace Foundation, New Delhi, 1981 (mimeo).

Banerjee, P., "Development of Skills and Attitudes in Basic Education", http://ignca.nic.in/cd obu 19 htm

Bantock, G.H., T.S., Eliot and Education, Faber and Faber, London, 1970.

Barbar, B., "Is Bloom Right", Span, June 1988.

Barbara, Tint, "Peace Education in India: Academics, Politics and Peace", *The Canadian Journal of Peace and Conflict Studies*, Vol. 39, Nos. 1-2 (2007) pp. 23-37.

Basu, A.K., Nai Talim: Need of the Hour, *Ailaan*, Vol. II, Issue 11.

Beloo Mehru, New Race Aims of True Education: Sri Aurobindo and Mahatma Gandhi, April 2011.

Bharathi, K.S., *Thought of Gandhi and Vinoba*, Concept, Delhi, 1995.

Bhattacharya, S., The Contested Terain, Perspectives on Education in India.

Bhole, L.M., *Collected Papers in Gandhian Thought*, Amani International Publishers, Kiel, 2007.

Bhole, L.M., *Essays in Gandhian Socio-Economic Thought*, Shipra Publications, Delhi, 2000.

Bhole, L.M., Gandhi's Hind Swaraj, Shipra Publications, Delhi, 2015.

Bonner, T.N., "The Unintended Revolution", *Span*, September 1987.

Burns, H.W. and C.J. Brauner (eds.), Philosophy of Education: Essays and Commentaries.

Center for Research and Innovation, Alternative Educational Futures in the USA and in Europe: Methods, Issues, and Policy Relevance, OECD, 1972.

Chakravarty, P., "Similarities and Differences in the Educational Principle of Shri Aurobindo and Mahatma Gandhi", *VSRD Technical and Non-technical Journal*, Vol. 3(5) 2012.

Chandra Sudhir, "Gandhi Ka Swaraj", in Antim Jan, May 2013.

Chaube, S.N., *A Textbook of Educational Philosophy*, Wisdom Press, New Delhi, 2011.

Chaube, S.P., *Recent Philosophies of Education in India*, Concept, New Delhi, 2005.

Cholkar, Paraga (ed.), *Vinoba-Vichar, Dohan*, National Book Trust, India, New Delhi, 2002. (Hindi)

Chopra, Radhika, and P. Jeffery (eds.), *Educational Regimes in Contemporary India*, SAGE, New Delhi, 2005.

Coombs, H., *The World Crisis in Education*, OUP, 1985.

Coombs, P.H., *The World Educational Crisis, A Systems Analysis*, OUP, 1968.

Copley, A.C. and G. Paxton (eds.), Gandhi and the Contemporary World: Essays to Mark the 125th Anniversary, 92 (Gan) Gan, 181969.

Curren, Randall (ed.), Philosophy of Education: An Anthology.

Darji Chirag, "Educational Philosophy of Mahatma Gandhiji".

Darji Chirag, "Gandhian Outlook and Philosophy" (Details unavailable).

Darji Chirag, and Subba Rao, "Educational Philosophy of Mahatma Gandhiji" *Interdisciplinary Educational Research*, Vol. 1, Issue 4, 2013.

Darji Chirag, The Philosophy of Gandhi, Concept of Truth and non-violence.

Dharampal, The Beautiful Tree.

Divan, Kunder Balwant, Vinobanchi Vachne, Akshar Mala, Vareda, 1960 (Marathi).

Diwakar, R.R. and Mahendra Agrawal (eds.), Special Issue on Peace Education, *Gandhi Marg*, Vol. 6, No. 4 and 5, July-August 1984 (special issue).

Doyle, J.F., *Educational Judgements*, Routledge, London, 1973.

Druva Kumar, "Shiksha Ka Buniyadi Shastra" (Hindi), *Antim Jana*, February 2013.

Ekanath Easwaran, *Gandhi the Man*, Jaico, Bombay, 1997.

Elvin, H.L., Education and Contemporary Society, C.A. Watts and Co., London, 1965.

Everett Reimer, *School is Dead—An Essay on Alternatives in Education*, Penguin Education, Auckland, 1971.

Frankana, Philosophy of Education.

Furth, M.G. and M. Wachs, *Thinking Goes to School*, OUP, London, 1975.

Gandhi, M., "Education As per Mahatma Gandhi", *Sevagram Sevak*, 15 February, 1942.

Gandhi, M.K., (ed. By Bharatan Kumarappa), *Towards New Education*.

Gandhi, M.K., Mangal Prabhat, Navjivan, 1997.

Gandhi, M.K., *Towards New Education* (ed.) Bharatan Kumarappa.

Gandhi, Vinoba, Ivan Illich, Frerre, Huxley, Vivekananda, Aurobindo, Ravindranath Tagore, A Comparative Study on Gandhiji's own education.

Gandhi's Educational Philosophy for the 21st Century, http//www, May 28, 2013 (Tuesday).

Gandhiji, "NT ki or" (ed.) By Bharatan Kumarappa, Navajivan Prakashan Mandir, Ahmedabad, 1956. (Hindi)

Gangul A., and Gangul R., "Gandhian Philosophy of Education in Twenty-First Century" (Details unavailable).

Ganihar, N.N., and B.B. Police Patil, Tagore's Philosophy of Education, Global Vision, New Delhi, 2013.

Ghosh, S. (ed.), Faith of A Poet, Bhartiya *Vidya* Bhavan, Mumbai, 1964.

Ghosh, S.C., The History of Education in Ancient India (c. 3000 BC to AD 1192, Munshiram, Manoharlal Publishers, New Delhi, 2001.

Glenn Langford, *Philosophy and Education, An Introduction,* Macmillan, London, 1968.

Humayun Kabir, *Education in New India,* George Allen and Unwin, London, 1956.

Ivan Illich, *Deschooling Society,* Penguin, 1973.

Jain Shilpa, Gandhiji's Nai Talim vs. NCRT's National Curriculum Framework for School Education (details not available).

Jeffreys, M.V.C., The Aims of Education Pitman Education Library, London, 1972.

Kamla Dwivedi, *Gandhiji Ka Shiksha-Darshan,* Shri Publishing House, New Delhi, 1986. (Hindi)

Kanigel, R., "Technology as a Liberal Art", *Span,* March 1989.

Kilpatric, W.H., Philosophy of Education.

Knaeba, J., Experiments in Moral Sovereignty Friends of the Gandhi Museum, Pune, 2006.

Kneller, G.F., (edit), *Foundations of Education,* John Wiley, London, 1971.

Kokandakar, J.R., *Aims of Education,* Bhavan's Book University, Mumbai, 1999.

Krishnakumar, "Gandhi's Nai Talim", Samyayoga Sadhana, Oct. 1, 2004.

Kuldip Kaur, Education in India (1781-1985), Policies, Planning, and Implementation, CRRID Chandigarh, 1985.

Kumarappa, Bharatan, Basic Education, 1951.

Laurence, J.C., *Educational Thoughts,* Rajat Publications, New Delhi, 2010.

Lucas, C.J., *What is Philosophy of Education,* The Macmillan, London, 1969.

Mahadevi Varma, "Shikshak AAtmashodhan" in Nai Talim, Uttar Pradesh Acharyakul Sammelan Anka, December 1970, pp. 213-2407.

Mahatma Gandhi for Twenty-First Century, Oxford, 2008.

"Mahatma Gandhi on Education" (Author name not available).

Manju, Bharatiya, *Shiksha Padhati and its Problems,* Omega, 2009.

Margaret Cole, "Gandhi The Man", in S. Radhakrishnan (ed.), *Mahatma Gandhi 100 years,* Gandhi Peace Foundation, New Delhi, 1968.

Natarajan, Minakshi, "Jadopar Chot", *Antim Jan,* May 2013 (Hindi).

Mishra, A. and others, *Gandhian Alternative to Contemporary Problems*, Abhijit Publications, Delhi, 2004.

Murphy, S., *Why Gandhi is Relevant in Modern India*, Gandhi Peace Foundation, New Delhi, 1990.

Myrdal, G., *The Challenge of World Poverty*, A Penguin International Edition, 1970.

"Nai Talim", Wikipedia, The Free Encyclopedia.

Ngugi va Thyongo, "The Imperialism of Language", in *Antim Jana*, May 2013 (Hindi).

O'Connor, D.J., Introduction to the Philosophy of Education.

Pandey, J. (eds.) *Gandhi and 21st Century*, Concept, New Delhi, 1998.

Panikkar, K.N., "India's Education Policy, from National to Commercial", *EPW*, April 23, 2011.

Pankajam, G., *Pre-Primary Education: Philosophy and Practice*, Concept, New Delhi, 2005.

Paranjape, M.R., "The Relevance of Mahatma Gandhi's Educational Policy for the 21st Century," Website, May 2013, 28-13.

Parel, A.J., *Gandhi's Philosophy and The Quest for Harmony*, Cambridge University Press, 2006.

Peter, R.S. (ed.), Philosophy of Education.

Phenix, P.H., Philosophy of Education.

Philip Joseph, "Mahatma Gandhi's Concept of Educational Leadership", *International Journal of Economics Business and Management Studies*, Vol. 9, No. 2.

Prabhu, R.K. and Rao, V.R., The Mind of Mahatma Gandhi, Navajivan Trust, 1969.

Prakash Ved, "Concerns about Autonomy and Academic Freedom in Higher Education Institutions, *Economical and Political Weekly*, April 16, 2011.

Prasad Ambica, *Life and Philosophy of Mahatma Gandhi*, Cyber Tech Publications, New Delhi, 2012.

Radhakrishnan, S. (ed.), *Mahatma Gandhi*, Jaico, Mumbai, 1998.

Rajput J.S., Gandhi on Education, http://www.nete-India.org/pub/ Gandhi/ Gandhi-2htm

Rajput, J.S., Gandhi on Education, National Council for Teacher Education, Mimeo, 1998.

Raley, Philosophy of Education, In the Era of Globalization.

Rao, K., "Educational Philosophy of Mahatma Gandhi and Swami Vivekananda—A Comparative Study", International Referred Research Journal, October 2010.

Reid, L.A., Philosophy and Education.

Reimer, E., School is Dead: An Essay on Alternatives in Education.

Richards, G., Gandhi's Philosophy of Education, 37.01/Ric, 193953.

Russel, B., *On Education, especially in early childhood*, Unwin Publishers, London, 1926.

Saidin, K.G., *Bharatiya Shikshanik Vichardhara*, Minakshi Prakashan, Meerat, 1969.

Shankar Vijayvargiya, *Bhartiya Shikshaka Itihas*, Rajpal Publishers, Delhi, 2003. (Hindi)

Sharma, Namrata, *Value Creators in Education*, Regency, New Delhi, 1999.

Sharma, S.D., *Shiksha, Disha Aur Drishtikone*, Pravin Prakashan, New Delhi, 1996. (Hindi)

Sing, J.P., *Vinoba's Utopia of the Future Indian Society and Education*, Indian Publishers, Delhi, 1999.

Singh, Y.K. (ed.), *Educational Philosophy of Mahatma Gandhi*, APH Pub. Corp., New Delhi, 2009.

Sorabji, R., *Gandhi and the Stoics*, OUP, 2012.

Sujit Sinha, Rethinking Nai Talim, What Roles can Universities Play?

Sykes, M., *Education in Search of a Philosophy*, Earthcare Books, Kolkatta, 2013.

Sykes, M., The Story of Nai Talim: Fifty years of Education at Sevaram, India (1937-1987).

Tagore, R., *Lectures and Addresses*, Macmillan, Mumbai, 1980.

Tagore, R., *Personality*, Macmillan, 1917.

Thomas, N.V., "Mahatma Gandhi's views on Education: With Special Reference to "Nai Talim" or "Basic Education", *The Journal of Sophia Asian Studies*, No. 29, 2011.

Tilak, B.G., Education Policy in India in transition. *Economic and Political Weekly*, March 31, 2012.

Tripathi, S., *Gandhi's Philosophy of Education*, Anmol Publications, New Delhi, 2007.

Tripathy, M., *Bhartiya Shiksha ka Vishva Kosha*, Omega Publications, Delhi, 2007, Vol. 1 to 5.

UNESCO, World Education Report, 1995.

UNESCO, World Information Report, 1977/98.

Unto Tahtinen, *The Core of Gandhi's Philosophy*, Abhinav, New Delhi, 1979.

Upadhyaya, J.M., *Mahatma Gandhi: A Teacher's Discovery*.

Varkey, T.N., Mahatma Gandhi's Views on Education with Special Reference to 'Nai Talim' or "Basic Education", *The Journal of South Asian Studies*, No. 29 (2011).

Ved Prakash, "Concerns about Autonomy and Academic Freedom in Higher Education Institutions," *Economic and Political Weekly*, April 16, 2011.

Vijendra Kumar, *Vashishta, Bharatiya Shiksha Ka Itihas*, Arjun Publishing House, New Delhi, 2003.

Vimla Rao, "Gandhi and Ruskin on Education" in *Gandhi and the West*, University of Mysore, Mysore.

Vinoba Bhave, Acharyakul, Maharashtra *Sarvodaya* Mandal, Gopuri, Wardha.

Vinoba, *Shikshan Vichar (Marathi)*, Paramdharma Prakashan, Pavanar, 1965.

Vinoba, *Vinoba Sahitya (Hindi)*, Vols. 1 to 21, Peramdharma Ashram.
Wilson, J., Preface to the Philosophy of Education.
Wingo, G. Max, *Philosophies of Education, An Introduction*, Sterling, New Delhi, 1975.
Woods, R.G., Barrow R.C., *Introduction to Philosophy of Education*.